SACRED JOURNEY

gift of Earth and Spirit

*Purchased with funds from the
Morris J. Wosk Memorial donation*

Robert C. Wild

CANADIAN MEMORIAL UNITED CHURCH
1825 WEST 16th AVENUE
VANCOUVER, BC
V6J 2M3

Cover Design by Margaret Cameron

Order this book online at www.trafford.com/07-1511
or email orders@trafford.com

Most Trafford titles are also available at major online book retailers.

© Copyright 2007 Robert C. Wild.

All rights reserved. No part of this publication may be reproduced, stored in a retrieval system, or transmitted, in any form or by any means, electronic, mechanical, photocopying, recording, or otherwise, without the written prior permission of the author.

Note for Librarians: A cataloguing record for this book is available from Library and Archives Canada at www.collectionscanada.ca/amicus/index-e.html

Printed in Victoria, BC, Canada.

ISBN: 978-1-4251-3799-1

We at Trafford believe that it is the responsibility of us all, as both individuals and corporations, to make choices that are environmentally and socially sound. You, in turn, are supporting this responsible conduct each time you purchase a Trafford book, or make use of our publishing services. To find out how you are helping, please visit www.trafford.com/responsiblepublishing.html

Our mission is to efficiently provide the world's finest, most comprehensive book publishing service, enabling every author to experience success. To find out how to publish your book, your way, and have it available worldwide, visit us online at www.trafford.com/10510

Trafford PUBLISHING

www.trafford.com

North America & international
toll-free: 1 888 232 4444 (USA & Canada)
phone: 250 383 6864 ♦ fax: 250 383 6804
email: info@trafford.com

The United Kingdom & Europe
phone: +44 (0)1865 722 113 ♦ local rate: 0845 230 9601
facsimile: +44 (0)1865 722 868 ♦ email: info.uk@trafford.com

10 9 8 7 6 5 4 3 2

Grandfather,

Look at our brokenness.
We know that in all creation
Only the human family
Has strayed from the Sacred Way.

We know that we are the ones
Who are divided
And we are the ones
Who must come back together
To walk in the Sacred Way.

Grandfather,
Sacred One,
Teach us love, compassion, and honor
That we may heal the earth
And heal each other.

Ojibway Prayer

PREFACE

During most of Gaia's existence of about four billion years, our home planet has taken excellent care of herself. In recent decades, however, we have been learning that human activity is causing major disruptions to Earth's integrity. A major task we face is to discover how to live in a healthy relationship with a healthy Earth.

When I ponder this challenge, my mind turns not only to policies and programs but also to the roots of human behaviour. Our humanly devised plans to remedy the ecological crisis - even the best of them - can be vitiated by the same kinds of human failings which in the past have resulted in thoughtless and harmful exploitation of Earth. And this reminds me of a story I read years ago.

The English novelist John Galsworthy tells of a certain Russian kulak who was a prosperous farmer constantly seeking to expand his land holdings. His neighbours asked him, "How much more land do you need?", and after some thought the man said, "As much as I can walk around in one day". When challenged to show how much this might be, the man chose a day with the most hours of daylight and prepared himself as thoroughly as he could. He set off promptly at sunrise. His neighbours watched as he strode at a fast pace around his chosen route, pressing himself to his maximum walking speed. As sundown came close, he increased his pace so as to be sure to return in time to his starting point where his neighbours were gathered. Exactly at sundown he arrived, and fell down dead.

The title of the story is "How Much Land Does a Man Need?", and the answer is: sufficient in which to bury him. But the story addresses a much deeper and more pertinent question: What will happen to a society as it moves beyond a subsistence economy and is able to provide itself with material abundance? How much will prove to be enough? Galsworthy seems to suggest that this is a question of moral values and of priorities in human life. The greedy man in the story failed his test. If humanity fails its test, the only Earth left will be one in which we shall be buried. What, then, is the alternative?

We are capable of good deeds, both personal and social, which have deep roots in spiritual and moral qualities originally seeded in Western culture by different aspects of Hebrew, Greek and Christian teaching. And in the last century we have been listening responsively to wisdom from other great religious traditions. We must rediscover and reaffirm - sooner rather than later - those creative and compassionate energies we require to transform our current dysfunctional thoughts, feelings and actions.

In this book I name and describe some of the natural energies we have as children of Earth. I discuss the beautiful mystery of soul in the human which is crafted so as to be constantly renewed by the sublime and universal Mystery of the Sacred. I advocate recovery of spiritual and moral resources of such depth and durability as can provide a foundation for the social and ecological values and actions needed for the healing of Earth and all her creatures.

Traditional religions picture Heaven as our blessed destiny and Earth as our temporary home. But when we reflect on the new cosmology that is rooted in the discoveries of science, and bring this cosmology into dialogue with our religious inheritance, a new and different story of spiritual meaning and beauty emerges. We learn that Earth is our sacred home. We learn that this home is the gift of the Sacred Presence in whom Earth and all its creatures have an unknown destiny within the Mystery of the unfolding universe. And, for the present, we are content to discover a Sacred Journey given to us so that we may become who we are called to be, by both Earth and Spirit.

This book is written as a sequel to "Sacred Presence: in Search of the New Story",* and there is some overlap between the two texts. However, in writing this book I have not assumed familiarity with the other.

Robert Wild
Autumn 2007

Salt Spring Island, BC
V8K 1B6
<wildacre@saltspring.com>

* Trafford Publishing, Victoria, BC, V9B 5Z3
   on-line publishing: 1-800-232-4444
                   <sales@trafford.com>

TABLE OF CONTENTS

A TIME AND A TASK — page 1

THE WONDER OF SOUL — 8

  Soul in Encounter with Others
  Soul in Vulnerable Exchange
  Soul as Creator
  Soul and Spirituality
  Spirituality and the Cosmos
  Soul and Sacred Presence
  A Tale about Soul

A SPIRITUAL JOURNEY — 29

  Soul work
  Growing in Faith and Life
  Sacred Presence as Companion
  To Know and Live our own Truth
  Humans and Earth

VOICES FROM THE JOURNEY — 48

  Earth is our Sacred Home
  The Psalmists' Passion
  The Art of Wool-gathering

THE COSMOS, THE SACRED and a NEW STORY — 91

  Traditional Symbolism of the Sacred
  A New Cosmology
  Immanence and Transcendence
  The Divine Intiative
  Religionless Christianity
  A New Paradigm
  A New Story
  Moral Peril and Signs of Hope

EPILOGUE — 120
APPENDIX - Eucharistic Liturgy — 123
BIBLIOGRAPHY — 130

A TIME AND A TASK

We in the western world have rushed eagerly to embrace the future - and in so doing we have provided that future with a strength it has derived from us and our endeavours. Now, stunned, puzzled and dismayed, we try to withdraw from the embrace, not of a necessary tomorrow, but of that future which we have invited and of which, at last, we have grown perceptibly afraid. In a sudden horror we discover that the years now rushing upon us have drained our moral resources and have taken shape out of our own impotence.
(Loren Eiseley, "The Firmament of Time")

In our time there is a sharply growing awareness that people have put Earth in peril and that Earth's peril brings with it a threat to human well-being. A recent radio report tells that the Yangtze River, third longest in the world, is drying up and that an important inland Chinese city is threatened with severe water shortage. This is yet another sign that climate change is upon us. Increasing ice melt will bring the disappearance of many significant glaciers, perhaps as soon as mid century, removing the source of much of the water which sustains human habitation.

The roots of this threatening calamity are not environmental - they are spiritual and moral. Wherever human population has been most dense, people have been unable or have deliberately refused to live creatively and compassionately with one another, and in a respectful and responsible relationship to Earth. After each humanly devised disaster - such as extensive and repeated acts of deforestation - we have said, "We can do better, we have learned our lesson". But the response to each historic failure has seldom been sufficiently truthful, and our renewed aspirations for better personal and social living have never been strong enough to correct our willful behaviour. We have continually deceived ourselves.

In recent decades it has become dramatically apparent that the cost of this repeated deception is being paid by every creature on Earth and by Earth herself. We no longer have anywhere to hide, no longer any possibility of deceiving ourselves. Because we are enemies to one another, and because we have been callously indifferent to the living ecosystem system that supports us through its countless sub-systems, we have become enemies of Earth.

This is not to deny flashes of wisdom, creativity and beauty in the human story. There have been many episodes in which the best of our nature has been revealed in acts of generosity and compassion, has been expressed in great insight and achievement. And some of these achievements, if only for a limited time, have had significant positive results for Earth and brought material well-being to humans. But in the large centres of population we have never been able to sustain for long that gentle fashioning of human relationships which brings health and renewed life to Earth.

Ronald Wright ("A Short History of Progress", 2004) traces how, over several thousand years of human history, different cultures in several parts of Earth developed so as to end in a 'progress trap'. Each society which he discusses took its own economic activity beyond the point of being in balance with the forces of nature, tipping the balance and creating a 'trap' which ended its life. He does not always discuss the human factor in detail; but where he does, a fundamental failure in human relationships is evident as a central cause of the collapse. Patterns of domination in the human scene have overflowed into human destruction of the natural order.

For over thirty years we have watched economic activity become increasingly global in structure and move us toward global cultural homogeneity. The domination of some nations over other nations, and of a relatively small elite in each nation over its own large majority, are continuations of long-standing and widespread practises of self-assertion and self-aggrandizement. Familiar patterns of social and environmental destruction continue and there is no end in sight. David Suzuki, noted scientist and environmentalist, recently likened humanity to a train full of people fighting over who will have the best seats while the train itself is hurtling toward a solid brick wall.

If we turn to humanity's great religious traditions for help, the history of past performance is not encouraging. I am well acquainted only with my own Christian tradition and must leave it to others to speak for theirs. But it seems to me that the central thrust of the words and deeds of Jesus of Nazareth still waits to be heeded by a majority of Christians. For example, one of his central precepts is found in the Gospel of Mark 9:33,

> Then [Jesus and the twelve] came to Capernaum; and when he was in the house he asked them, "What were you arguing about on the way?" But they were silent, for on the way they had argued with one another who was the greatest. He sat down, called the twelve, and said to them, "Whoever wants to be first must be last of all and servant of all."

Even the earliest Christians seemed unable to understand and accept what Jesus is reported to have said on that day in Roman Palestine. The history of the church displays a consistent neglect of the precept of servanthood to one another.

In opposition to Jesus' teaching we find widespread patterns of human self-assertion, a desire for power over others, and the accumulation of personal wealth. These characteristic marks of human relationships have been dominant throughout most of human society during the last 6000 years. They have created a predictable succession of elite ruling classes and an equally predictable succession of oppressed subject peoples. Until the recent rise here and there of a middle class (a blink of time in the history of Earth), one tenth of each society has regularly impoverished nine tenths. And a corollary of this repeating social pattern has been the exploitation of nature. Maltreatment of humans brought with it devastation of the natural environment and vice versa!

Throughout this long and sad history of human violence in our relationships with one another and with Earth, most religions of the world have taught and worshipped violent gods, heavenly power-brokers who were believed to control the fate of Earth. And this consistent element in religious teaching prevailed even when religion also urged love and compassion as key virtues for human relationships.

There is, for example, a central paradox in the Christian Bible. Its closing document, "The Revelation of John the Divine", presents the Lord God as coming in righteous judgment in the Last Days to destroy a sinful world through cataclysmic acts of violence. The four Horsemen of the Apocalypse are messengers of the divine wrath. And this document is placed at the end of the Bible to complete other writings which contain themes of a divine love in creation, and of love among humans for one another. Christianity has always had this schizophrenia in its belly - as witness the present resurgent preaching of apocalyptic violence by the church's contemporary conservative wing.

If humanity is to have a long-term future on Earth, we shall need to become much more vigilant in affirming the elements in our religious traditions which can enable creative relationships with one another and with Earth.

In this book I hope to participate in a task which others have also taken up. The challenge is to seek a creative spirituality and an ethical vision which can help humans to heal themselves and Earth. We need a spirituality, ethics and morality based in a new vision and understanding of the cosmic Sacred Presence which is the Heart and Meaning of all things. What humans have in the past meant by 'God' must now be transformed in line with our knowledge of the amazing universe that science is showing to us. If we do not change our theology and our spiritual practice, and discover moral imperatives which flow from these changes, we shall not have the ability to live in harmony with one another and to befriend Earth and all her creatures.

In advancing, elaborating and defending this thesis I do not wish in way to diminish the importance of the many practical programs being advanced by responsible people who seek to correct how humans live on Earth. Dramatic reductions in the use of petroleum products; a thorough revision of forestry practises; moderating how we fish Earth's waters; reductions in human patterns of consumption in the wealthy nations - these and related efforts must continue to be urged. But such programs and policies are not likely to notice nor take into account the present spiritual and moral blindness in human society, nor how that blindness impacts negatively on the natural order.

The task of this small book is to name the spiritual roots of the human adventure and to discuss how these roots might be nurtured so as to serve the well-being of humans and of Earth. This task needs the attention of many minds and hearts in order for a groundswell of spiritual creativity to rise everywhere. We are all pilgrims in a Sacred Earth, and collectively we have a profound spiritual potential with which to serve its true destiny.

This book discusses the relationship of the mystery of the human soul to the Mystery of the Sacred - a Mystery which is both hidden and disclosed in every dimension of the universe. And I will look again (as I did in a previous book) at the revolution in religious awareness which has already begun and waits to be completed. Finally, I explore some ways in which we can open ourselves to the divine Presence and accept the grace to become non-violent people who are learning to love Earth in all that we do.

I do not believe that we can easily or completely reverse the present distortion of natural forces which threatens to cripple Earth as a beneficent habitat for the human race and other species. It seems that in the foreseeable future there will be some planetary downturns which are now unavoidable. No one seems to know at present whether or how or when these destructive trends can be stopped or reversed.

Some of us, however, are learning from the new cosmology being developed by science and are revising our basic convictions about the origin and meaning of Earth and of our place in it. We are learning to listen to Earth for a wisdom rising out of its own Truth. We are working to renew our spiritual and moral lives. We are responding positively to the challenge of Eco-theologian Thomas Berry who calls us to re-invent the human.

Many people today are questioning the religious traditions they inherited and are seeking spiritual renewal. The way is open for us to seek a new relationship with the Sacred Presence, and to find there a gentle optimism for living in the uncertain times ahead. We might even become a healing presence in a world that is desperately sick.

Questions for Discussion

The thoughts presented in this book are open-ended. I invite you to ponder them and use them to promote conversation with your friends.

In this opening chapter there are two clusters of ideas and feelings: one is apprehensive and the other hopeful. I am apprehensive about humanity's ability successfully to overcome our destructive actions in relation to the environment, but I am also aware of the human potential for generosity, compassion and justice. I am apprehensive about human tendencies towards self-assertion and a desire for status, and about social pressures which lead us to desire an ever-increasing material standard of living. But as a Christian I find in Jesus of Nazareth an affirmation of creative spiritual and moral qualities for which we all have the potential. Where do you stand in this negative/positive polarity?

So many of our contemporary problems manifest themselves in social sickness. Why is it that we know many good persons and yet are confronted by widespread social patterns and forces which are destructive?

Ronald Wright's book demonstrates how entire societies have been led to a dead end by their elite classes. Where do we find the spiritual resources to change the historic patterns in society of misguided elite power, and to create communities in which every voice has a realistic opportunity to influence the directions we want to take together?

Every enduring society has had its Great Story, its creative 'myth' which is grounded both in historical experience and in fruitful imagination. These Stories have encouraged and enabled people to dream and to build creative communities (remember Martin Luther King, "I have a dream ..."). What ingredients do you imagine might belong in the New Story that our world needs now?

What elements in our Christian nurturing might help us to contribute to the building of the New Story? What elements in that nurturing should we leave behind?

THE WONDER OF SOUL

*So God created humankind in his image,
in the image of God he created them;
male and female he created them. (Genesis 1)*

The ancient Hebrew poetic cosmology which contains the above verses is usually dated to the sixth century BCE. Another, much earlier and quite different version of the creation of humanity is found in Chapter Two of Genesis: "Then the Lord God formed the earth creature from the dust of the ground, and breathed into its nostrils the breath of life; and the earth creature became a living being." As the anthropology of the Bible developed over time, the "breath" became identified as 'soul' in the human, a spiritual presence in each of us presumed to come as a creative gift of the Lord God and making us "in the image of God".

With the emergence of the scientific method in Europe beginning in the sixteenth century, doubt began to grow about this attribution to human beings of soul (as distinct from mind), since there appears to be no empirical evidence for its existence in the body. One resourceful researcher weighed a human body immediately before and after death and reported no difference in weight, declaring that this proved soul didn't exist! Indeed, the word 'soul' is not commonly used now even in religious discourse; it has yielded place to the discussion of 'spirituality' as an attribute of each person and to the affirmation of 'spirit' as in some manner a dimension of the human psyche. But in what follows I presume that we cannot do without this word soul and all that it signifies, and I hope to provide a general description applicable to this term which is reasonable and useful.

Soul is both hidden and disclosed. Much of the evidence of soul as disclosed has been drawn from the study of religious experience. Within this work, a precise description of soul - the 'still point' - is lacking and probably always will be. The evidence is all indirect. We make deductions from our deepest, most intangible and sometimes very powerful life experiences; but these tell us nothing of the hidden soul-in-itself. However, even as we acknowledge this limitation, this lack of precise definition of soul, we continue to need our stories, our metaphors and symbolic language which will allow us to speak with useful meaning about the hidden depths of our nature. Periodically these depths disclose themselves to us, and usually when we least expect it. Here is an example of what I mean.

The year 1980 was an unexpected pause in my usually busy life. As is sometimes true of such pauses, I was faced with a painful break from the past and a need to consider my options for the future. I decided to travel. I joined the Canadian Youth Hostelling Association, purchased a pair of sturdy boots and backpack, and late that spring found myself in the south of Europe. I had become a wanderer on a pilgrimage with no fixed destination.

On one particular morning, after a very rough and uncomfortable overnight bus ride through the Croatian mountains, I arrived at 8 am in the city of Trieste, Italy, at the northern end of the Adriatic Sea. I checked my backpack in the train station and secured a ticket for onward travel leaving that evening. A helpful lady provided me with a map of city walks which could take the visitor to various important sites. Though I was tired and in poor spirits, I set out in the cold drizzle to find the cathedral. This meant a long uphill climb from the dockyards during which I lost my way and ended up at a large parish church cared for by Franciscan priests. A sign on the door told me that the building was closed to visitors between noon and 3 pm. It was now 11:45 am, but I went in anyway and sat down on a pew in the semi-darkness.

I looked into myself. I was seeking to connect with God, Nature, my own soul, other people - anything; but I found only a void. Internal emptiness. I felt lost and defeated. I heard the footsteps of a man approaching. A silent priest tapped me on the shoulder, led me quietly to a door and, seeing me out, shut and locked the door behind me.

I sank down to the worn stone stoop. As I leaned back against the door I felt like trash which had been swept out onto the street. I sat and wept. When I had regained my composure I walked a short distance to sit upon a wide stone fence. I ate some of the sardines, cheese and bread that I always carried with me. Gradually I felt the soul that had so recently seemed irrevocably lost was being restored to me as a gift and a trust. The surrounding world greeted me with its beauty, and I thought of a text in Genesis: "then the Lord God formed man of the dust from the ground."

There is no explanation for that kind of experience. But in its own way it certified to me the painful and joyful mystery of the soul's journey.

SOUL IN ENCOUNTER WITH OTHERS

From our earliest moments after birth, and continuing through all our days, we experience ourselves as both 'object' and 'subject' in the context of a surrounding community of persons. We feel like an object whenever an outside force seeks to manipulate us. This manipulation can come from a familiar person, a stranger, a public body or policy - in fact from any force which seeks in any way to downgrade our self and its interests.

On the other hand, we feel like a subject when we are consulted about our interests, when we are listened to with respect, when our actions and opinions are valued. Treated as an object, our sense of self is diminished; treated as a subject, our sense of self is enhanced. A positive and growing sense of self as subject comes to us as a gift within creative relationships with others and with the world at large. The feeling of possessing a distinct, purposeful, valuable and valued 'centre' - the self as subject - has traditionally been named an experience of soul.

As children, some of us populated our private worlds with other personalities who existed as projections of our own thoughts and feelings. We created a small and intimate world in which the self could live safely, a kind of early rehearsal of the interpersonal work we would be doing all our lives. By the normal skills of imagination and play, through naming and other devices, we bestowed value and meaning on dogs, cats, birds . . . on toys and other beloved objects/subjects, all of which together formed a close and safe environment for ourselves. We bestowed subjectivity indiscriminately on these living and non-living creatures and thereby formed a community within which we could live securely for shorter or longer times. We created a personal world in which we encountered the 'other' with complete safety because the other was a part of ourselves. The soul was thus its own instructor in a world of personal imagination; our sense of self as subject grew as we probed our feelings and thoughts by projecting them outward upon these intimate others.

Experience gained in the intimate personal and social worlds of childhood normally overlaps and interlocks with experience we accumulate through a widening encounter with the world. The world out there offers us different kinds of encounter which constantly hold surprises and in which the self as subject is variously challenged, delighted, afraid, unconcerned, pained, damaged, rejected . . . and so on. In some of these encounters, especially those in which we permit ourselves to be vulnerable, we are aware that we are changing, that soul is in some manner able to respond creatively and joyfully to the external world. This happens, for example, when we open ourselves to the natural environment as it delights and enriches us.

On the other hand, there are encounters which we carefully try to control or avoid. We learn that personal choice is possible. We decline reciprocity, we decide not to be involved, we try to keep certain kinds of encounter to a minimum. We are learning that we can choose our friends, that we can decide which activities we enjoy and which we feel are not appropriate for us.

There is pain as well as happy discovery in this process, in these experiences which bring a new kind of maturity. Life is not smooth nor simple; the world of human personalities is complex, challenging and often dangerous. By repeated experiences we learn that soul is malleable in its encounters with others, and we discover that often we do not have much control over this inner plasticity. A self as subject is growing, and some of that growth is in the hands of other people, both for good and for ill.

In our world of 'others' it is important to become aware that everything in the universe is inter-connected.

> To be is to be related, for relationship is the essence of everything. In the very first instant [of the evolution of the cosmos] when primitive particles rushed forth, every one of them was connected to every other one in the

entire universe. . . For galaxies too, relationships are the fact of existence. Each galaxy is directly connected to the hundred billion galaxies of the universe, and there will never come a time when a galaxy's destiny does not involve each of the galaxies in the universe.

Nothing is itself without everything else. Our Sun emerged into being out of the creativity of so many millions of former beings. The elements of the floating presolar cloud had been created by former stars and by the primeval fireball. The activating shock wave would have been ineffectual but for the web of relationships within the galactic community.

(B. Swimme and T. Berry, "The Universe Story")

It is vital that we understand soul 'relationally'. You and I - all people - are expressions of myriad inter-connected relationships which extend into the furthest dimensions of the universe. Try to imagine yourself, to feel yourself, as knit into a cosmic web which moment by moment confers value and meaning upon your self and upon an infinite number of 'others'. The microcosm of each person's immediate neighbourhood is simply the specific place where we can learn to discover and give local expression to these universal values and to this common meaning.

SOUL IN VULNERABLE EXCHANGE

One of the clearest ways in which we experience soul is through intentional self-disclosure. Each person has a core of experiences, thoughts and feelings - a cumulative history of the self as subject - which is basic to our sense of who we are. We value this secret personal core of felt meaning and we guard it with the greatest possible care so that it will not be violated by other people. And if by chance this violation does occur, we experience anguish and interior suffering. On the other hand, when another person's active loving invites us to share some of our self through self-disclosure, and when this is done safely and received graciously, our sense of self as subject is validated and deepened. We experience the kind of personal affirmation which is directly related to a healthy growth of soul.

We learn from experience when and how we are vulnerable to being damaged or diminished, and there is no formula to help us. The best we can do is to avoid negative situations and any blaming of our self or others for these encounters when they do occur. However, as we learn how to use our vulnerability creatively, this quality of soul opens us to unseen depths of the world around us. We become able to accept beauty and ugliness, joy and sorrow, well-being and suffering, goodness and evil, and we grow in spirit. Our vulnerability is the basis of 'empathy', our ability to 'feel with' others in experiences of truth-full exchange. Within such creative exchange soul is radically open to the other and we experience mystery in the relationship. Intentional, willing vulnerability can open us to dimensions of mystery.

Probably the most widely celebrated experience of this kind is 'falling in love'. The experience is so vivid that it changes our lives. But we are not precisely certain of what it consists; we grope for actions and words to tell of the mystery of loving into which we have been taken and are unable to express adequately what we feel.

Artists use our openness to mystery to share with us their works of painting, sculpture, music, drama, literature and architecture. Works of profound artistic worth draw us into an exchange with them of soul depth; they move us inwardly in unaccountable ways. We can have the same kind of experience with people and with the natural world around us; and sometimes in the richness of all this experience we come upon an aesthetic quality that we name 'beauty'. Also, through our openness to mystery we can recognize within human behaviour the moral quality we name 'goodness'. And yet again, in other experiences, we may believe that we have met the intellectual quality of 'truth'. However: not the awareness of beauty, nor of goodness, nor of truth, can be arrived at nor explained by any process of reasoning. In each of these exchanges between soul and others, our awareness is enriched by dimensions of mystery which are gifts facilitated by soul.

In fact, our lived world is comprised of a series of continuing, unavoidable and inexplicable encounters with others. And when we pause to reflect on this fabulous accumulation of experience, we find ourselves unable to number its variety. We are greatly satisfied and enriched by these gifts mediated by our openness to mystery. As it is, we can only respond deliberately to a tiny fraction of our world. By personal acts of attention, recognition, naming and valuing we gain only a limited feeling and knowledge of the extensive gifts we receive in our encounters with 'the other', with whatever in the cosmos touches us deeply.

SOUL AS CREATOR

It is not unusual for people to experience a special thrill which comes with a genuine act of creating. It may be a work of art, an unexpected good deed accomplished, successful baking of a delicious item, a new and original thought ...... the list of possibilities is limitless. And in each of these times we experience our interior creativity and know again something of our true worth.

Assistance in understanding the depths of this kind of experience comes as a spin-off from the science of quantum mechanics. Mathematical physicist and cosmologist Brian Swimme demonstrated this in a classroom lecture. He discussed the radical change experienced by some physical scientists in their understanding of what is 'real', of what we consider to be 'fact', when they were measuring the motion and location of the smallest particles of matter. Commonsense awareness leads us to declare as 'fact' what our five senses report to us. But, as Swimme reports, about seventy years of scientific research shows that there is an inescapable element of indeterminacy in what our senses tell us about the world around us.

As an example, Swimme proposed to his audience that they consider a sunrise. Suppose that four photographers each took a camera and on a given day in a certain location they all photographed the same scene of the sun rising over the horizon. We would not have four identical pictures. Even if this experiment were done an indefinite number of times, by any number of photographers, we would never have two identical pictures of that event. And the reason is simple: each camera receives its image of the sun rising over the horizon from a specific location and as a result of one particular photographer's aesthetic judgment. No two images can ever be identical because no two photographers are identical persons and no two photographers can be in one specific place at the same time.

If we change this example from the actions of a camera and photographer, and consider simply the factors in human awareness of a rising sun, we note that each observer looks out from a unique personal history, imagination, value system, etc. Therefore, because of each person's 'existential situation', the experience he or she calls 'sunrise' is always unique. The manner in which each person sees and names the scene is particular to them. What is seen and named by each person is the result of certain material factors in the atmosphere, in combination with the observation contributed by the person who gives it the name "sunrise". Each seeing eye, computing mind, and responding soul will have its own experience of that display of form and colour. The material situation is real enough, but *what that situation actually is for each person* is the result of its impact on one entire human physical and psychic awareness. No two people standing together experience the same sunrise.

What is 'real' for us is always a construct, involving both some objective situation and our knowing self. Recent decades of experimental work in the science of quantum mechanics confirm that the results of perceiving and knowing are always relative to the observer: that is, the process of observation influences what is being observed. For the human, we cannot know beforehand every detail of what we now observe. There is always an element of surprise.

As a result of this characteristic process, the lived world that each of us holds within the self has an accumulating, unaccountable and indeterminate quality which eludes our understanding. I will name the process 'open to mystery'. Moreover, as we discover how deliberately to exercise our openness to mystery, we learn to treasure its results.

In our continuous encounter with the world, our capacity for reasoning raises the expectation of intelligent understanding and clarity of meaning. On the other hand, to be open to mystery causes us to have experiences (the frequency varies with each person) where our normal exercise of reason is unexpectedly suspended. At such a time we are being invited to 'pause'. We wonder and we wait. The moment of mystery never yields its secret to the effort of investigation but, as we wait, there may be an unexpected gift. Whatever is present in this moment remains hidden until and unless it is able to give itself to us in voluntary self-disclosure. To wait in the moment of mystery is to be humbled.

A common occasion for this kind of experience is an encounter with something that strikes us as unusually beautiful. We gasp, our eyes open wider, and we become still. Awareness of the 'other' momentarily supercedes our self-awareness, and we receive an unexpected gift.

I have been once to Rome, during which I went three times to the great basilica of St. Peter. I came away from the first visit of about an hour puzzled because I was completely unmoved. This feeling was repeated after a second visit, though I did marvel at the magnificent architectural achievement. After the third time I wrote in my journal, "this time I felt the power of the place. I wonder why it took me so long?" Patience with ourselves is essential for the great experiences of life.

Regardless of how carefully we itemize the elements of our awareness in the 'now' - in the present moment - we are unable to predict precisely what will be the content of the next moment. Any given moment, as it arrives, will contain things amazing or trivial, interesting or not memorable, significant or unimportant. And this indeterminate element in our experience is normal, inevitable and potentially life transforming for us and for others. When we were children it provided us with a lovely sense of wonder and called forth our delightful powers of creative imagination. As adults we feel enriched when our openness to mystery brings unanticipated blessing into our lives.

Some time later in the European pilgrimage to which I referred above, I was traveling by train through Holland. As I gazed out the window I found myself recollecting some of my recent experiences and I was filled with an overpowering sensation of gratitude. I took up my journal and made the following entry:

> My soul rejoices in all things which come to me. That leaf, that butterfly, the women shopping, the man in the field, the child in the pram, the Mass priest, the cobbler in his shop. ALL, all is mine, and I am theirs. For I am a beggar, owning nothing and yet having all things. And I am God's and God is mine; for I am the poorest of the poor and the Holy One comes to fill me - I, who do not forbid the Coming but seek to welcome the soul's Light and Life.

Soul was within that moment, hidden at the Centre. And it was disclosed to me through my encounter with Earth and some of her beautiful creatures. The words I wrote rose up from soul because of its openness to mystery in all things, in its openness to Sacred Presence.

SOUL AND SPIRITUALITY

Within this multitude of encounters we are constantly being invited to soul work. We are being invited to understand and name for ourselves the content of what is being disclosed in these exchanges so as to rejoice in it and to receive its riches. If we accept the opportunity, we become participants in an ongoing and deeply personal process of integrating into one seamless stream of consciousness the various fruits of our acts of attention, recognition, naming and valuing. This process, and how we express its results in our daily living, is our 'spirituality'.

A person's spirituality is a complex and creative process of soul. As we learn about it and accept its significance, we realize that our spirituality marks the whole person and all that we do. It is a kind of synthesis of our aesthetic, intellectual and moral powers which, as we have already seen, enable us to be open to mystery. Moreover, a mature spirituality is capable of mystical experience, an activity which is not uncommon and not paranormal. Evelyn Underhill, in her comprehensive survey of the subject, says that "mysticism is seen to be a highly specialized form of the search for reality, for heightened and completed life, which we have found to be characteristic of human consciousness."

It is the mystics who encourage us to enter into the paradoxical nature of communion between Sacred Presence, which is Absolute Mystery, and the human soul, which is of Earth. They teach that "The All is The One, and The One is the All". In opening ourselves to The One in whom we can learn to trust, we simultaneously are present to The All who is beyond our comprehension. In this simple manner they affirm one of life's most astonishing possibilities.

Mystics come in all sizes and shapes and degrees of wisdom. Here are three beautiful examples of mystical writing:

> Fish cannot drown in water,
> Birds cannot sink in air,
> Gold cannot perish
> In the refiner's fire.
> This has God given to all creatures:
> To foster and seek their own nature.
> How then can I withstand mine?
> (Mechthild of Magdeburg, 13th century)

> Those who dwell, as scientists or laymen, among the beauties and mysteries of the earth are never alone or weary of life. Whatever the vexations or concerns of their personal lives, their thoughts can find paths that lead to inner contentment and to renewed excitement in living. Those who contemplate the beauty of the earth find reserves of strength that will endure as long as life lasts. There is symbolic as well as actual beauty in the migration of birds, the ebb and flow of the tides, the folded bud ready

for spring. There is something infinitely healing in the repeated refrains of nature - the assurance that dawn comes after night, and spring after winter.
     (Rachel L. Carson, "The Sense of Wonder")

Once

In a while

God cuts loose His purse strings,

Gives a big wink to my orchestra.

Hafiz

Does not require

Any more prompting than that

To let

Every instrument inside

Go

Berserk

("Hafiz, The Great Sufi Master"
     trans: Daniel Ladinsky)

  Gerald May ("The Dark Night of the Soul"), writing about the teaching of John of the Cross and Teresa of Avila, two 16th century Spanish mystics, says:

> When Teresa and John speak of the soul, they are not talking about a thing a person has, but who a person most deeply is: the essential spiritual nature of a human being. . . . For them, the soul is not a separate part or aspect of a person, but rather what you see when you look at a person with spiritual eyes.

  Though soul is commonly associated only with human consciousness, May suggests that we should recognize soul as a single, permeating and sustaining presence throughout our entire physical/psychic nature. The traditional division between soul and body is no longer tenable: the human is a single body/mind/soul unity who lives as one integrated organism within and in response to the cosmos. Soul in the human species is the name we give to our unique capacity for spirituality. It is an amazing fruit of the evolutionary process and permeates the whole of us. With the astonishing emergence of soul in the the species *homo* we find humanity's defining characteristic and our most sublime depths.

By its wondrous activity, soul gives a quality to all our mental and bodily functions, a quality which is unique among the creatures of Earth. In us, spirituality becomes a functioning element within the interdependence of everything in the entire cosmos, whether for good or for evil - both outcomes are possible from the exercise of our spiritual nature.

SPIRITUALITY AND THE COSMOS

The human species brings a unique contribution to the continuing evolution of planet Earth. This is our awareness of the spiritual dimension of life and a consequent responsibility for actions rising out of this awareness. There may well be other creatures - both on this planet and in outer space - which also bring awareness of the spiritual dimension of the cosmos into the flow of the evolving universe, but as yet we do not know of them.

For example, other Earth mammals do not have a finely developed moral sense which allows us to know good and evil and requires us to act from that knowledge. (Research with some higher primates indicates a rudimentary moral awareness, but it is not as developed as in the human.) The human experience of moral choice and of its consequences gave rise to the ancient myth of Adam and Eve in the Garden of Eden. In that myth, the human experience of being tempted to choose evil rather than good is symbolized in the serpent's words. And when Adam and Eve allow themselves to be tempted to do evil (to eat the forbidden fruit), they experience a changed relationship with Earth. They experience alienation from their natural home. This myth withstands the erosion of time because it speaks an enduring truth about us.

Our moral awareness and consequent experience of moral choice together form one of our special, if ambiguous, gifts to the universe. We also contribute to the cosmos our ability to imagine an open future. We have visions and values which can guide us in future relationships with one another and with the natural order. As the only species with a conscious openness to mystery and to the wide range of actions which this makes possible, we are able to bring our creativity to the service of planet Earth for its well-being. Through our spirituality we have a unique potentiality to enrich the whole created order - or to cripple it, and perhaps fatally.

Given the present state of Earth's ecology, we may question whether the coming of *homo sapiens* has proven to be the blessing it seems to promise. Our misuse of the unique capacity for intentional choice has caused the normal functioning of Earth's vital systems to suffer disastrous interference. Some careful observers ask now whether we may have taken the planet to a point where certain dynamic forces of destruction cannot be stopped. At the very least, this possibility should lead us to re-examine what we are doing with the unique gifts that we have received.

SOUL AND SACRED PRESENCE

Bishop Augustine of Hippo, North Africa, in the early 5th century gave an arresting statement about one work of soul in a prayer:

> Thou hast made us for thyself
> and our hearts are restless
> 'til they find their rest in Thee.

In company with a wide variety of people of his own and other times, Augustine became aware of a sublime Mystical Reality permeating the entire cosmos. He believed that soul (heart), with its openness to mystery, constantly seeks fulfillment in communion with the Universal Mystery. All religions agree that soul's highest achievement is to enter into an Exchange of Love with the Divine. We seek, however inadequately, an intentional communion with the Holy One, with the uncreated Mystery of Sacred Presence.

There are many traditional forms of quiet reflection in which soul seeks to enter into self-disclosing communion with the Divine. This practice is partly gift and partly the reward of our deliberate efforts. It involves the risk of naming our innermost feelings and desires as truthfully as possible; it means becoming naked before the Holy One.

The degree of inner freedom and wisdom that we have for this kind of self-disclosure is supported by the level of certainty that we have of being loved unconditionally. The more certainty, the more self-disclosure is possible. A high degree of certainty is dependent on previous positive experiences of the divine Loving.

Sometimes this interior reflection takes the form of a confession of heart-felt moral fault; sometimes reflection involves a delight in one's own being - a self-affirmation which is often difficult to share with another human being. But in whatever form this kind of self-awareness and self-disclosure occurs, the result is a strengthening of communion between the soul and the Divine.

The loving that is received and expressed in a relationship with the Divine grows and deepens only as it is also being expressed in self-giving service in the world. Without such service, our desire to love the Holy One loses its integrity. "Those who say, 'I love God', and hate their brothers or sisters, are liars.'" (1 John 4:20)

Sometimes formal religious practice interferes with the development of a natural desire for intentional communion with the Holy One. The adventure of growing in faith can be short-circuited by the substitution of unthinking adherence to religious dogma for a genuine and personal spiritual pilgrimage. We can become a victim of second-hand religion. Consequently, an enquiring agnosticism is often the safest entry into the religious quest because religious establishments of all kinds, in search of converts, have closed systems of belief which can pre-empt challenging and creative soul work.

Formal religious practice of the dogmatic variety is widespread and is an affliction rather than a blessing for the planet. There is strong evidence, for example, that this practice has stolen and is continuing to steal from us our creative potential to serve the well-being both of humaniity and Earth. By substituting narrow religious ideologies for the creative life and work of soul, dogmatic religions cause strife among people and serious injury to Earth's living systems. It is to be hoped that deliverance from this spiritual sickness may yet come from the authentic restlessness of which Augustine writes, from an urgent willingness to take up open-ended and careful soul work.

A TALE ABOUT SOUL

This is the moment of a human birth.
During some undetermined prior event,
Soul had saturated the emerging embryonic organism
> to become its 'within', its interior depth and truth -
> a mysterious emanation of the Sacred.

Body grows,
and Mind within the complex convolutions of the brain.
Body/Mind is being shaped by Soul from the raw physical
> to become a person.

Soul delights in self-expression through the Body/Mind.
And now, in birth,
Soul begins its journey into the expansive world
> through a multitude of connections.

Soul/Body/Mind
connects ever more deeply with Mother Earth and her creatures,
> connects with other souls.
And Sacred Presence deepens Its communion with the new person.

Physicality is the foundation,
Soul is the genius,
and Mind brings growing self-awareness to the integrated person
> of Soul/Body/Mind.
The Universe fosters in the person wisdom and imagination,
> a feeling for Beauty and a search for Truth.

In birth, this Soul/Body/Mind enters the Earth Community and begins to take on a social character. Through its increasing range of connections, the new person grows a character, a personal history. It is as though an entity that begins colourless gradually acquires from its context rich hues of every conceivable shade; as though a surging potential acquires increasing form and depth - the contours of an emerging person.

The person has the possibility of sharing her whole reality with others; she possesses a unique spiritual 'density' that is palpable - if we care to notice it. She yearns to bless the world. But, sadly, she also experiences limits on what she is able to share (there are blocks to this work). Then the whole Earth Community suffers a loss.

Some people - scattered here and there over Earth - acquire a remarkable depth and density of character, and they become for the rest of us an unusual presence. To use paradoxical language: they have 'substantial' spirituality. One infallible mark of a substantial soul is humility, of which the 12th century monk, Bernard of Clairveau, tells us there are several 'degrees'. Bernard expects many of us to reach the lower levels of his degrees; but Thomas Kelly, in "A Testament of Devotion", writes about the highest:

> Humility rests upon a holy blindedness, like the blindedness of one who looks steadily into the sun. For wherever that person turns her or his eyes on earth, there they see the sun. The God-blinded soul sees naught of self . . . but only the Holy One.

This degree of humility is soul's most wonderful achievement on

Earth; it enables gentle and wise persons to come among us who can lead us into Truth. If we are fortunate and attentive, we may know one or two such persons during the course of our lifetime. Each one is a special gift of the Sacred.

Questions for Discussion

When was the first time you can remember having a sense of a 'centre', a Still Point, and what was that experience like?
What was the event or circumstances that provided this disclosure?

How would you describe the experience of creativity? If you remember an element of mystery in this kind of experience, what can you say about it?

What do you do intentionally to open yourself to experiences of beauty, or truth, or goodness?

If you would like to, name some aspects of what you consider to be your spirituality.

To what extent do you find yourself drawn toward mysticism? What in this work attracts you?

To what extent do you have a feeling of belonging to the universe? How would you describe this experience? What degree of awareness do you have of contributing yourself to the inter-connectedness of the cosmos, and what does this mean to you?

How would you describe the task of trying to integrate your personal spirituality with that of a community of faith to which you now belong, or to which you would like to belong?

What are some Names, Symbols, Images, etc. that help you to be present to the Sacred?

A SPIRITUAL JOURNEY

Blessed be you, mighty matter,
   irresistible march of evolution,
reality ever new-born; you who,
   by constantly shattering
our mental categories,
   force us to go ever further and further
in our pursuit of the truth.

Blessed are you, universal matter,
   immeasurable time,
boundless ether, triple abyss
   of stars and atoms and generations;
you who by overflowing and dissolving
   our narrow standards
or measurements reveal to us
   the dimensions of God.
      (Pierre Teillard de Chardin)

Life begins to be experienced as a spiritual journey when increasing self-awareness opens a way for intentional choice and invites us to live by it. This awareness can come at almost any age, and when it comes and is expressed in a new commitment, life is never the same again.

In our earliest years we experience life as 'given', as not yet open for serious questioning. Forces around us and within us shape the person we are becoming. Our family, the wider society and its cultural norms, the schools we attend, the groups we join - these give important input to our young lives. They establish the quality of our early years and lay down the foundations of our personality. But as we approach the teenage years we normally begin to wonder about choice, about which decisions we must learn to make for ourselves and how we might be able to make them.

This opening up of life can be closed off quickly, however, if the circumstances of adulthood move in on us so as to minimize our alternatives. Some people experience a radical loss of freedom at this time because a circle of pressing responsibilities snuffs out the possibility of making real choices. Other people enter the adult years with so little intentional shape to their lives that it seems impossible to make purposeful decisions. Under circumstances such as these, it is difficult to imagine a spiritual journey in the sense of being able to make important decisions about the future. But between the option of a generous personal freedom of choice and a nearly complete lack of it, there usually remains space in which to discover and put to use the leverage we actually have for making personal decisions.

The contemporary consumer culture of the West works constantly to discourage a spiritual journey. Not only are the basic values of this culture crassly materialistic and de-personalizing, seductive advertising by industry and commerce seeks to make our decisions for us and to discourage the development of discrimination in our judgments. However, if we wake up to these restrictive patterns and their destructive work, we can challenge them and reclaim our human right of personal choice.

SOUL WORK

The spiritual journey is unlike any other we might take. Other journeys commonly have perceived goals; this journey has no specific personal future in sight and we don't need one. Instead, we discover that the path of the spiritual journey is not ours to determine; it is provided as we travel. Our constant teacher is the divine Spirit and we journey with good intention and strong hope because our divine Companion is trustworthy.

The journey requires spiritual awareness and knowledge of ourselves that is supported by quiet reflection and a willingness to make thoughtful decisions. The fruit of the journey is an education and enlargement of soul, and a deepening experience of soul as guiding our daily choices. The relevance of our personal journey for the wider issues of interpersonal relations and community living, of social justice and world peace, becomes expressed in growing spiritual vision and in wiser and more responsible decisions and actions.

Though by its nature the journey occurs within us, it is constantly reflected into the world around because the interior life becomes evident in our behaviour. Who we are affects other people through what we do. And if we are alert, we shall notice returning messages from them, both direct and oblique, which assist our self knowledge and enrich our journey.

For pilgrims of the Spirit's Way, the central measure and test of the interior life is the standard of neighbour love: "How does the divine love abide in anyone who has the world's goods and sees a brother or sister in need and yet refuses help?" (1 John 3:17) "If the neighbour in need is not constantly in our prayer, then that prayer is not Christian" (Brother Roger, of the Taizé Community). The interior and external aspects of our lives are inter-dependent.

Earth is also a 'neighbour' to whom many people have been giving renewed attention in recent decades. There are programs and policies being suggested in many quarters for the complex task of discovering how humans can live in creative relationship with the natural order. These are indeed essential at community, municipal and national levels - but we need more than technical solutions. We need worldwide spiritual renewal within which many people become capable of new vision and transformed actions in their relationship with Earth. We must find new ways of living on Earth that respect its sacred character. Without spiritually dedicated people, I doubt that our economic, political and technological programs of reform will be adequate to save Earth from ecological disaster. We need people of 'mindfulness', a quality which Buddhists seek to develop.

The spiritual, ethical and moral elements in human life are intended to grow in mutual support. If we fail to keep them in close relationship, our spiritual interests tend to become an escape from social responsibility and ethical and moral life loses clarity, motivation and bite. On the other hand, when our spiritual roots are nourished in partnership with ethical vision and moral endeavour, the spiritual life stays crisp and grounded and our behaviour draws conviction and energy from healthy spiritual roots. Human spirituality looks both outward to the world in compassion and active loving, and inward to the enlivening Sacred Presence hidden within everything.

> What you do not live, you cannot understand.
> What you do not understand, you cannot live.
> To be held by Truth and to live truthfully
> are interdependent and mutual.
> Neither advances alone,
> each advances with the other
> or not at all.

GROWING IN FAITH AND LIFE

The spiritual journey enables us to make intentional choices to foster spiritual, ethical and moral growth and these become expressed in appropriate action. To discover which choices are necessary and be able to act accordingly, we may be helped by using a path of 'Seek, Wait, See.' This is a simplified way of describing a method which is found in different forms in several traditions.

By 'Seek' I mean using daily reflection to review aspects of our life journey which are central for us at any given time. I think of questions such as: How do I think of the Sacred, now? Who am I in relation to this Presence? Who am I in relation to family, close friends, work associates? Who are the people and what are situations that seem to require a loving response from me now? At which points in my life do I want to become more intentional in Christian discipleship? It is not necessary or wise to try to address all our questions at one time; one or two will present themselves as work for any given day. As we recognize and record what our mind and heart tell us in response to such questions (a brief written record, often called 'journaling', is a definite help), we are directed to different kinds of soul work. In this work we respond to an invitation to 'seek'.

As we address a specific soul question over an extended period of time, both by thought and action, we may discover the need to 'Wait'. To wait is to realize that, in relation to this particular part of our seeking, a way of understanding or action that we previously found helpful and productive is no longer so. We have an experience of stumbling, of becoming aware of losing our way in this part of our intentional caring and living. To wait is to find darkness where before there was light. And in response, we exercise close attention to what our mind and heart tell us, but without being able to draw conclusions. We wait, and we do not withdraw from this work. This is time for a special kind of patience with our self. Important hidden work is going on that may take considerable time to mature before its meaning can be disclosed to us.

By 'See' I mean being moved from darkness to light, from uncertainty and confusion to clarity. When we 'see', we experience a surge of energy. Gratitude comes with new understanding and we move on in this part of our journey. It is important to write something for our self about this experience.

As we follow the dynamics of 'Seek, Wait, See' we find ourselves being encouraged repeatedly to try new ways of thought and action, and we learn that we need never fear to make mistakes. It is very much a process of trial and error: to venture into new ways of thinking and acting always risks making mistakes. But when we stumble, we can usually make adequate amends for the faulty steps taken and make the necessary changes. The only failure we must always guard against is failing to hold ourselves responsible to follow through somehow on clear feelings and thoughts which we have gained in reflection - even though some of these will later be revealed as mistaken. In the spiritual journey, we are constantly moving from the self already known to us, to become the person previously hidden and waiting to be disclosed. We are persons in process, a work that finds its inspiration and strength in gifts from Earth and Earth life, and from Sacred Presence.

As mentioned, the simple steps of 'Seek, Wait, See' are drawn from classical teachings. Specifically, there is much in the traditions about spiritual desolation and consolation that is compressed into the words 'Wait' and 'See'. The soul is led into darkness (desolation) where, unknown to ourselves, we are being made ready to receive truth (consolation) which can never be discovered by our own efforts alone. Here the Mystery of Sacred Presence directly engages the mystery of soul. In times like this - which recur regularly for those who persist in their journey -

'to wait' means to trust in the divine Loving as we engage in the creative struggle of soul.

I once heard this time of waiting as likened to traveling in a train through a long tunnel. Entering the tunnel we gaze out the window into the pitch black and feel as though we are not moving at all. But when the train emerges from the tunnel we suddenly see that we have indeed moved a considerable distance. We see a new landscape, different from that which we left behind.

As we participate over time in the path of 'Seek, Wait, See' we we become dogged and persistent in the journey. But now and again this Way is anything but dogged: we are taken unexpectedly into a 'moment of grace'. Such a moment might be as simple as a small, startling insight into our daily living which comes as though out of nowhere, something important for the journey that we had not recognized before. It might be a sudden shift of consciousness as we speak with a friend, an unanticipated awareness of the gracious divine Loving. Or a moment of grace might arrive with an abrupt awareness of a personal fault previously unnoticed. We realize that in one aspect of our life there is a way of thinking and acting that needs to change. And this brings with it a desire for spiritual growth, a desire which we need to articulate clearly for ourself. We feel a distinct assurance that a specific interior transformation and a better way of living is being offered to us, no matter how long it may take to be realized fully. But whatever its provenance and whatever
its degree of surprise, a moment of grace brings spiritual enlightenment to our journey and a new moral imperative into our living. Two example may help to illustrate this.

I grew up in a large extended family. Both among my own folk and in school playgrounds I often heard a rich variety of expletives, curse words, obscenities, blasphemies, and similar excesses of speech. They were, for me, part of normal life, a way of speaking that I absorbed as being natural. Only later as an adult did I awaken unexpectedly one day to the fact that I had never chosen this language for myself, and that this very day was the opportunity to make a decision to begin the change. For the first time I realized that it matters a great deal how I express my reaction to unpleasant surprises, bitter frustrations, painful difficulties. And although I may never be completely reformed, the direction in which I chose then to move is right.

The other example of a typical moment of grace is common to many people. We stumble upon, hear or read about the plight of a person or group of people and we realize we are being challenged to respond. There may be some initial hesitation but the commitment to action is not in doubt. This is beautifully illustrated in a story told by G.K. Chesterton in his account of the life of Francis of Assisi.

> Francis was riding listlessly in some wayside place, apparently in the open country, when he saw a figure coming along the road towards him and halted; for he saw it was a leper. And he knew instantly that his courage was challenged, not as the world challenges, but as one would challenge who knew the secrets of the heart of a man. . . . Francis Bernadone saw his fear coming up the road towards him; the fear that comes from within and not without; though it stood white and horrible in the sunlight. For once in the long rush of his life his soul must have stood still. Then he sprang from his horse, knowing nothing between stillness and swiftness, and rushed on the leper and threw his arms round him. It was the beginning of a long vocation of ministry among many lepers. for whom he did many services; to this man he gave what money he could and mounted and rode on.

Each moment of grace supports the loving purposes of Sacred Presence in human life. They come in unexpected forms and in any time or place or circumstance.

Meanwhile, the journey of faith continues as we endeavour through spiritual and moral endeavour to occupy the 'space' between who we are now and who we are becoming. We are constantly being led on from the point to which we have come, urged by the Spirit to continue with as much commitment and wisdom as we possess. And we do this willing to give the time and effort required to fulfill our God-given desires. These desires are often at first rudimentary and not fully formed; they may even be incorrectly understood. What is certain is that we must not let go of the little we have seen and we must respond actively to each new intimation of the next step in our journey. The process is its own reward.

This is the path of growing in faith, hope and love. And though there are astonishing moments of grace, the basic rhythm is undramatic and calls for self-discipline in our spiritual practice. The interior life develops slowly within us. From a tender shoot it grows to become a stronger plant yielding understanding, courage and generosity. And ultimately this trio matures into believing, hoping and loving.

SACRED PRESENCE AS COMPANION

In the long history of Judeo-Christian spiritual traditions there is repeated testimony both to the hidden presence of the Holy One and to divine self-disclosure. In the Hebrew Scriptures we find stories of disclosure to Abraham and Sarah, Isaac and Rebecca, Moses and Miriam, Elijah, Isaiah, Amos and others; in the Christian Scriptures we find stories of disclosure to Jesus, Paul and other members of the early church. Here is an example from the stories about Elijah, a story richly embroidered with the mythology of Hebrew storytelling.

> The word of the Lord came to Elijah, "Go out and stand on the mountain before the Lord, for the Lord is about to pass by." Now there was a great wind, so strong that it was splitting mountains and breaking rocks in pieces before the Lord, but the Lord was not in the wind; and after the wind an earthquake, but the Lord was not in the earthquake; and after the earthquake, a fire, but the Lord was not in the fire; and after the fire, a sound of sheer silence. When Elijah heard it, he wrapped his face in his mantle and went out and stood in the entrance of the cave. Then there came a voice to him and said, "What are you doing here Elijah?"

Preceding this event, Elijah had displeased Queen Jezebel with his proclamation of a discomforting "Word of the Lord" and she had run him out of the country. As a result, he was deeply discouraged about his prophetic commission. But after the encounter on the mountain, Elijah knew that he was being instructed to return to his appointed task. When Sacred Presence chooses to be revealed as our Companion, this has explicit consequences for the person being addressed.

During the nearly two thousand years of Christian church history, we find a succession of notable teachers of the spiritual life each with stories to tell of divine self-disclosure. These events were always unanticipated and unannounced and they occurred within the normal and continuing experience of the Divine as hidden. Classical terminology names these periodic occasions of disclosure as experiences of 'active grace', and the on-going interior strength to continue a life of faithful discipleship as the gift of 'habitual grace'.

One of the outstanding voices testifying to both habitual and actual grace is Julian of Norwich, an English anchoress of the 14th century. Julian lived alone in a simple enclosure attached to a church wall where she was consulted by many people who treasured her wisdom. We know of her through writings labeled simply, "Showings". Here is a famous passage from this work:

> Our good Lord . . . is our clothing, who wraps and enfolds us for love, embraces us and shelters us, surrounds us for his love, which is so tender that he may never desert us. And so in this sight I saw that he is everything which is good, as I understand.
>
> And in this he showed me something small, no bigger then a hazelnut, lying in the palm of my hand, as it seemed to me, and it was as round as a ball. I looked at it with the eye of my understanding and thought: What can this be? I was amazed that it could last, for I thought that because of its littleness it would suddenly have fallen into nothing. And I was answered in my understanding: It lasts and always will, because God loves it; and thus everything has being through the love of God.
>
> In this little thing I saw three properties. The first is that God made it, the second is that God loves it, the third is that God preserves it. But what did I see in it? It is that God is the Creator and the protector and the lover.

Julian's witness to the divine loving as constant and dependable speaks of the habitual grace by which her daily discipleship was sustained and which she acknowledged and claimed by faith. Her story about the hazelnut reveals that she also had moments of active grace, of inexplicable divine companionship, in which her understanding was suddenly illuminated and her heart filled with joy.

The spiritual journey, we learn, is sustained both by the quiet gift of faith which is daily sustained in our spiritual practise and also by astonishing experiences of divine self-disclosure. Of these experiences there are countless examples in the history of religions. The stories are distinctly individual in nature because each addresses a unique personal journey.

However, some common characteristics can be identified. There is no claim to have 'seen' the Presence. Self-disclosure of the Sacred is never of the Mystical Reality in Itself, but only of Its effects on the subject. (There may appear to be exceptions in the stories, but only because mystical symbolism is used in the telling.) Divine self-disclosure is always unanticipated and is initially unaccountable and amazing. It is never the subject of boasting and is usually kept private unless there is good reason to tell of it. It often carries a moral imperative: something is to be done which was not previously seen. And finally, Sacred Presence revealed as our Companion is often mediated through the spirituality of another person.

One of the places I visited during my pilgrimage of 1980 was the Lake District in northeastern England. When leaving that region, I travelled south by a tourist boat on Lake Windermere to Bowness, intending to walk from there to the town of Kendal - a distance of about fourteen miles. I looked for and found a footpath sign indicating where I could walk overland but was soon dismayed when the 'path' gradually vanished from sight. A nearby, friendly farmer told me that - in spite of the presence of the sign - this path had not been in use for years! He advised me to walk the road.

The day was cool, overcast and drizzling, the pavement was not conducive to a pleasant walk, my backpack was heavy, and some of my body joints were complaining. The day was turning out to be miserable. By late afternoon I arrived at the upper end of a gentle downslope about half a mile long, at the far end of which was the town of Kendal. As I walked disconsolately toward town I noticed in the distance a dim figure moving up the slope. Gradually the figure developed into a person and then into a plump country woman carrying a loaded shopping basket. As she came close to me she stopped and began to speak: "May the road rise to meet you, may the wind be always at your back, may the sun shine strong upon your face and the rain fall softly on your fields. And until we meet again, may God hold you in the hollow of his Hand."

As she came to the end of her speaking, she reached over to me, put her hand on mine and with the brightest of blue eyes looking steadily into my own she said softly, "And may the Lord bless you". And then she was gone.

I have not before nor since felt so well blessed. A dismal day was transformed with light.

TO KNOW AND LIVE OUR OWN TRUTH

At the heart of the spiritual journey is a need to increase in understanding and appreciation of our personal truth and to live as faithfully as we can within that truth. Sometimes this is called living with integrity.

Other people give us names, usually without our knowledge. Silly, stupid, wise; beautiful, strange, ugly; active, lazy, passive; interesting, boring, shady . . . names beyond numbering are handed out by the world around us. So, how do I name myself? What names best disclose the inner person - names which I might prefer, for a time at least, that other people not know about? Names for the self that are discovered in the journey are precious gifts.

Since personality is dynamic, our personal truth is constantly evolving. How I named myself last year - or found myself being named within my own heart - will not necessarily be adequate to name myself today. But being open to these truth-revealing names is both essential and helpful. They disclose how I am to understand myself, now.

We use this special language about our selves primarily, but not exclusively, during our quiet times in the Presence. And even as we name ourselves, we are listening within for confirmation or dissonance in the words we use. We learn to observe which of our current names have become inadequate for the person we are becoming, names which must now be left behind. We listen for new words which feel more truthful, testing them continually both in our prayer and in our daily living. Rosemary Haughton has some excellent counsel for this work: "It is in the struggle to articulate truthfully that our words become capable of actually communicating truth".

Gerald May ("The Dark Night of the Soul") comments that "Teresa [of Avila] heard God's voice in prayer saying, 'Seek yourself in Me, and in yourself seek Me.'" This kind of seeking is possible only insofar as we are committed to name ourselves as truthfully as we can. Dietrich Bonhoeffer prays to his God, "Who am I before You, now?" This prayer should echo down each day, month and year of our lives. To live that prayer daily is to discover who we are becoming as a friend and companion of the Holy One, a person called to be open to other people and to be deeply respectful of Earth and all her creatures.

The process of discovering our names is not complicated nor strenuous and it is usually interesting. Many women discover depths of meaning for themselves in 'mother', and learn how to live into that name as a significant calling. To be a 'neighbour' can acquire special importance when it relates to a person for whom we have a demanding responsibility. To be a 'friend' can help to focus a relationship that is deepening. Ordinary words, discovered in times of reflection as applying to ourselves, can have new depths of meaning. They help us to become aware of and desire spiritual resources that we need to live faithfully. And when we are constantly open to receiving new names which help us to track our spiritual path, it is wonderful how these can suddenly appear. Here is an example.

Some years ago at the home of friends, my attention was drawn to a photograph of a Buddhist monk's hands. One hand was holding a book and the other a bowl. When I asked about the picture, I learned that the monk went daily out from his monastery, using his bowl to beg for rice and thus to receive his food for that day. Immediately I thought: "This then must be the meaning of the words in Jesus' prayer, 'Give us each day our daily bread'. Am I, too, a beggar who asks no more than enough for each day?" Two months later I reached the ecumenical community in Taizé, France. In that place of beautiful spiritual practise I knew that 'beggar' is a name I was to accept for myself. Since that time, over 25 years ago, I have pondered the truth of that name and tried to learn how I can live into it.

Another event that involved renaming myself - a 'moment of grace' - came in the early years of my journey. I had decided to begin a daily discipline of prayer and I acquired a pocket-size loose leaf binder and marked out different pages to designate different areas of concern I believed called for focussed attention. At that stage I knew almost nothing about daily prayer, only that it was something done by other pilgrims of the spiritual life. One page I designated as 'family', where - among others things - I placed the names of my five children. I decided to pray that one or more of them might be led into a monastic vocation. Each day I paused to hold this desire in my heart, until the day when I felt a serious dissonance within me. I erased the words (it is my habit to work with pencil and eraser!), leaving a blank which on each day following reminded me of the children but without indicating with what intention. Not many months later I became aware of the wording which belonged in the space: "That I might learn to respect and respond to the unique personality of each child." I knew then that my personal truth did not allow me to try to choose the children's futures. In more general terms, I knew that I must discover how to name myself in ways which urge me to be attentive to and supportive of the precious truth in each and every person I meet.

Incidentally, this is an early example of how my prayers asking God to do something for other people have been altered to become intentions which seek changes in myself for the better service of others.

HUMANS AND EARTH

In the mid 1990's I participated in a conference on social justice held at a centre administered by one of the First Nations in British Columbia. Early in the proceedings any persons interested were invited to participate in a sweat lodge ceremony, in groups of six to eight. Large boulders were being heated in a fire outside a small circular lodge made of branches and clay. After the heated boulders had been placed inside the lodge they were doused with water so that the lodge was filled with steam. The group inside sat on low benches around the steaming centre pit and the leader led several rounds of prayer during which each person could participate. The leader instructed us to conclude each of our prayer contributions with the words, "And all my Relations". Afterwards I learned that this phrase opened up our prayer to touch all the creatures of Earth.

I have often reflected on the significance of that experience, and I am still learning what it means to include Earth and all her creatures within the orbit of my spiritual awareness. The community of my spiritual life is actually much larger and much more inter-connected than I had been trained to acknowledge.

One of the main roots of the culture in which I was raised goes back 2500 years. At that time, the life of ancient Greece was at its most brilliant. From the Greeks, among many other legacies of that society, the Western world has learned the skills of analysis: to take things apart in order to discover how they work. Other cultures have made a similar discovery but Western society has taken that method of investigation and its consequences for planet Earth to their most extreme expression. Symbolized in the microscope, the stethoscope and the telescope, we have dismembered the natural world into its component parts and now are in peril of losing sight of the whole picture. We are seldom conscious of "All my Relations".

One over-riding task in our society for the immediate future, therefore, is to find a creative synthesis which can bring together in our understanding the artificially separated parts of our world. Thomas Berry says that "Earth is a communion of subjects, not a collection of objects." But we will not accomplish the task of understanding, experiencing and valuing this communion through even the most sophisticated analytical techniques that we might devise. This is a soul task - to be worked out through careful spiritual, intellectual, emotional and social endeavours. We need to imagine and create a future in which the natural and human worlds become blended into a single integrated whole. The kind of people capable of this task will be those who are engaged in intentional spiritual journeys, are open to gifts of Earth and Spirit, and are able to work with others in communities which serve the healing of both society and Nature.

The spiritual journey - soul's journey - is today more necessary than ever before. So many fundamental questions are being raised about the manner in which humans are living in the world that nothing less than use of our full powers will enable us to find solutions. These questions need spiritual wisdom and wise practise if we are to ponder, imagine and act creatively.

We live in the midst of ecological, economic and political crises of Earth-threatening proportions. We need a profound awakening of spiritual powers such as can come within a spiritual journey. Here, in this well-tested path, is a resource for the quickening of personal and public ethical vision and moral action by which to respond to the challenges we face as humans on this amazing planet Earth.

Postscript to this chapter:
For the reader who is beginning an intentional journey, I have two suggestions and a caveat.
Suggestion One. There are some general characteristics of the Way which are common to many of us:
   - plan a daily quiet time, beginning with not less than 20 minutes each, when you are alone and can become aware of the 'still point' where you are centred.
   - practise listening for the inner Voice.
   - clarify what you hear and are able to understand, and keep written notes.
   - form purposeful intentions to act in ways which give expression to what you are learning.
This much seems to be essential - but you may find other ways to shape your own practise and may discover other elements to be included.
Suggestion Two. Try to find a 'Companion of the Way'. Companions share experiences without making comparisons or judgments. It helps to have a soul friend who in listening gives

you the opportunity to verbalize what you are discovering and, in so doing, enables you to go more deeply into your experience.

And the caveat. We may choose to reflect carefully on what other people say about the spiritual journey - including what has been written here. But each person's path is deeply influenced by the unique qualities of her or his own life experience. We will do best by feeling our way carefully, without forcing our self into any particular mold. Be gentle with the soul.

Questions for Discussion

What actions are you already doing with some regularity which would be improved if you were 'intentional' about them? What personal values and commitments are you expressing when you do these actions?

Discuss 'Seek, Wait, See' and clarify this process where my description needs more elaboration. Share with one another other procedures that you already follow as you seek clarity for the journey.

What might we do to help ourselves when we "deliberately occupy the 'space' between who we are now and whatever is ahead for us"?

As you feel able, share experiences which were 'moments of grace' for you.

As you feel able, share experiences of divine self-disclosure. What ethical imperatives for your life, if any, were present in these disclosures?

What have you been learning about responsibility for the healing of Earth as a consequence of taking up an intentional spiritual journey?

VOICES

FROM THE

JOURNEY

EARTH IS OUR SACRED HOME

THE PSALMISTS' PASSION

THE ART OF WOOL-GATHERING

EARTH IS OUR SACRED HOME

Mountains can be understood as agencies in the world, participating in the ongoingness of the universe. That is, mountains act, and in multivalent ways. They sculpt the cycles of the hydrosphere and atmosphere. They shape the climates and thus the biology of the local region. And particular mountains also stun at least some of the animals. A human being, for instance, can climb a mountain and be hit by something so profound, at so deep a level, that the human will never be quite the same. This precise feeling will not occur on the ocean or in a cave or a valley. Other sorts of experience will take place there. This specific mountain moment will emerge only in the presence of the mountain; it is evoked out of potentiality by the mountain. The dynamic of the mountain is accomplishing something in the universe, is acting, is altering reality.
(Swimme and Berry, "The Universe Story")

From the moment of embryonic conception each person continuously gathers life as a gift from Mother Nature. Our bodies grow because of her generous provision for our physical needs; our mental consciousness is formed in response to everything that we see and hear and feel around us - including the stars which shine upon Earth. As Thomas Berry says, "It takes a universe to make a child." Can we imagine what stunted creatures we would be if we lived on the moon and if the furnishing of our growing bodies, minds and souls were confined to moon's bleak landscape? The richness of human life is the result of a profusion of gifts from Earth as she discloses herself to us in all her amazing fecundity.

But there is also mystery in planet Earth which offers a different kind of experience. This mystery humans have always sensed and sought; it generates the response of wonder, and sometimes of shock. It is a hidden truth which awakens mystical dimensions of the human mind. As Swimme and Berry testify, a human "can climb a mountain and be hit by something so profound, at so deep a level, that the human will never be quite the same."

The scientist James Lovelock proposed that Earth is a single living organism, a unified mega-organism composed of unnumbered interdependent living systems of every conceivable size and significance. 'Gaia' (the Greek Goddess of Earth) is the name he gave to this organism. So complex is Gaia that our best efforts to understand her provide us with comprehension of only a small fraction of her secrets, of her truth. And partly because of this long-standing ignorance of and indifference to this hidden truth, humanity violates the integrity of Earth. The present state of the physical environment is testimony to that indifference and to its unhappy consequences.

We can appreciate now why Aboriginal Peoples have consistently spoken of the need for 'respect' in our relationship to Earth. They understand and acknowledge that a humble deference to the sacred reality of Earth's being is essential for our own health and survival, and for the well-being of Earth herself. When we regard Earth simply as an object to supply our needs, we feel free carelessly to exploit her wealth. But if we regard Earth as a Subject to be respected, our attitudes and actions change (which is the reason I capitalize the word 'Earth' and prefer not to speak of 'the' earth).

There are many avenues which lead to a greater awareness of the mystery in Earth. The most obvious, and the most readily available, is to increase the extent and depth of our exposure to the diversity and subtlety, to the majesty and beauty and power in Nature. This avenue is open to everyone.

In the summer of 1980, backpacking my way across the south of Europe, I came to the medieval town of Dubrovnik on the Adriatic Sea. My second day there I took the twenty minute ferry ride to Lokrum Island, with a lunch in my small sack but my bathing suit left behind. I soon realized that this omission was a bad mistake since the sea there was warm, clear and inviting. So I was delighted when I saw a sign, "Nudist Bathing 500 Meters". The 'beach', it turned out, was solid rock reaching inland for a considerable distance and extending vertically at the edge about ten feet above the water. I joined picnickers on the 'beach', stripped, and entered the gently swelling water.

During that early afternoon I followed a simple routine. I dove into the water, swam for a while, climbed out on a rope ladder, and lay flat on the hot rock. Each cycle lasted about thirty minutes. I was overwhelmed by the immeasurable powers of Nature as they embraced my body: the sea lifting me, the rock holding and warming me, the sun baking me. I felt tiny. I felt gently surrounded and supported by these amazing forces.

Later I began walking slowly around the small island to return to the ferry dock. Unexpectedly I was halted on the path by an overwhelming sense of being loved by trees, shrubs, soil, insects, rock, sky, sea, wind, sun ....

I wept with the weight of the blessing.

A second avenue we can use to approach Earth's truth is by reading books and studying photographs which reveal investigations undertaken by the natural sciences, especially when the authors help us to reflect on Nature's hidden depths. (Molecular biologist Ursula Goodenough has written a fine book titled, "The Sacred Depths of Nature".)

A third avenue is to be found in poetry.

> To be of the Earth is to know
>   the restlessness of being a seed
>   the darkness of being planted
>   the struggle toward the light
>   the pain of growth into the light
>   the joy of bursting and bearing fruit
>   the love of being food for someone
>   the scattering of your seeds
>   the decay of the seasons
>   the mystery of death
>   and the miracle of birth
>
>   John Soos

Praise wet snow
      falling early.
Praise the shadow
      my neighbour's chimney casts on the tile roof
even this gray October day that should, they say,
have been golden.
                        Praise
the invisible sun burning beyond
      the white cold sky, giving us
light and the chimney's shadow.
Praise
god or the gods, the unknown,
that which imagined us, which stays
our hand,
our murderous hand,
                        and give us
still,
in the shadow of death,
      our daily life,
      and the dream still
of goodwill, of peace on earth.
Praise
flow and change, night and
the pulse of day.

                                  Denise Levertov

Gratitude to Mother Earth, sailing through night and day -
    and to her soil: rich, rare, and sweet
        in our minds so be it

Gratitude to Plants, the sun-facing light-changing leaf
    and the fine root hairs, standing still through wind
    and rain; their dance is in the flowing spiral grain
        in our minds so be it

Gratitude to Air, bearing the soaring Swift and the silent
    Owl at dawn. Breath of our song
      clear spirit breeze
        in our minds so be it

Gratitude to Wild Beings, our brothers, teaching secrets,
    freedoms, and ways; who share with us their milk;
    self-complete, brave, and aware
        in our minds so be it

Gratitude to Water: clouds, lakes, rivers, glaciers;
    holding or releasing; streaming through all
    our bodies salty seas
        in our minds so be it

Gratitude to the Sun: blinding pulsing light through
    trunks of trees, through mists, warming caves where
    bears and snakes sleep - he who wakes us -
        in our minds so be it

Gratitude to the Great Sky
   who holds billions of stars - and goes yet beyond that -
   beyond all powers, and thoughts
   and yet is within us -
   Grandfather Space.
   The Mind is his Wife.

     so be it.
              Gary Snyder (after a Mohawk Prayer)

WIND CHILD

They have just found where Monarch butterflies go
                            in autumn
those red-gold drifters edged in black
that blow like leaves but never
              quite coming to rest,
always fluttering
              a little out of reach,
                  disappearing
over the next house, or just making it
            above the hedge
flickering evasively through the last sunlight,
                the attrition tremendous,
                thousands die,
blown to sea, lost to children, lost to enemies but
                  beating, beating on,
speed fourteen miles an hour on a three-thousand mile
                        course to Mexico.

Where is the compass?
We don't know.
How did the habit start?
We don't know.
Why do the insects gather
in great clumps on trees
in the Sierra Madre?
We don't know.
They are individualists. They fly alone. Who wouldn't
in autumn
like to rock and waver southward like an everblowing leaf
over and through forests and hedges,
float in the glades
sip the last nectar?
What a way to go, you make it, or you don't, or the winds
snatch you away.
Fly Monarchs and then, if your wings are not too old
and frayed
start the long road back in the spring. Nature is
prodigal in numbers
prodigal of her milkweed children (did they learn to travel
from milkweed down?).
But I was overlooked, am really not human
would be first a tiger-striped caterpillar
and then a Monarch, elusive, flickering, solitary
blowing on storms and beating always beating
to go somewhere else, to another flower.
Over the fence then. Out of humanity.
I am a wind child.

Loren Eiseley

Teach your children
what we have taught our children -
that the earth is our mother.
Whatever befalls the earth
befalls the sons and daughters of the earth.
If men spit upon the ground,
they spit upon themselves.

This we know.
The earth does not belong to us,
we belong to the earth.
This we know.
All things are connected
like the blood unites one family.
All things are connected.

What ever befalls the earth
befalls the sons and daughters of the earth.
We did not weave the web of life;
We are merely a strand in it.
Whatever we do to the web,
we do to ourselves. . . .   Chief Seattle

The poems by John Soos, Denise Levertov, Gary Snyder,
    Chief Seattle, and the *Frontispiece* Prayer, are taken from:
   "Earth Prayers", E. Roberts & E. Amidon, eds.

The Poem by Loren Eiseley is taken from:
    "Another Kind of Autumn".

THE PSALMISTS' PASSION

In the Night Office [for three certain Sundays] let there be the singing of six Psalms and a versicle. Then lessons and their responsories . . . After these lessons let six more psalms with antiphons follow in order.
(The Rule of St.Benedict, Chapter Eleven)

Throughout the history of the Christian church, a central influence on its devotional practice has been the saying and singing of the Book of Psalms of the Hebrew Scriptures. An outstanding example is the regular use of the psalms in the seven Daily Offices of monasteries of the Benedictine tradition. But in fact all Christian religious orders and all the liturgical churches give the psalms a prominent place in public worship.

First impressions of that biblical Book, however, might make this steady liturgical usage seem strange and improbable. The psalms contain a great many explicit and/or subtle allusions to the history of the ancient Hebrews, and these references complicate the task for readers of later times and other places as we try to respond sympathetically to the texts.

Composed over several centuries, and often during tumultuous periods in the life of biblical Israel, the psalms reflect the specific circumstances of the authors - circumstances not necessarily known to readers of later times. And this difficulty is compounded today by the use of images of the Lord God which are inappropriate for many contemporary people. A clear example of the latter is the presupposition of most psalm Singers that Yahweh has chosen Israel for himself and that He (strongly male) is not the God of other nations.

For most of the centuries of church life, these complications have been eased for Christians by an unquestioned literal reading of the Scriptures as the inspired Word of God, a reading readily combined with a use of strong allegorical interpretation. This 'spiritual meaning' trumped any need for a critical approach to the text. Benedict's monks were little bothered by historical and cultural references in the psalms because they were not reciting the Psalter to learn about ancient Israel's national trials and tribulations, or her theological perigrinations. They sought to absorb and to reflect in their own lives the devotional fervour which is so evident in the psalms.

For more than a century now, however, all biblical literature has been subject to close critical study, including many excellent commentaries on the Book of Psalms. In the pages devoted here to a few of the psalms, I assume the validity of this critical work. And while I have personally benefited from this work and regularly refer to it in my own reading of the psalms, I am not concerned to explore it here. My purpose is closer to that of Benedict's monks: to notice and to appreciate how the texts can help to open the human soul to the mystery of Sacred Presence.

The 150 psalms can be classified under several distinct types. These include a majority designed for community liturgical usage such as thanksgiving, national lamentation, and covenant renewal between Yahweh and his people. Some psalms are intended specifically for use by Hebrew royalty, reflecting their special place in that people's national life and in their covenant traditions. Less than a third of the psalms are for individual use, and of these many are tied to situations peculiar to ancient Israel.

Only a small number of psalms are easily accessible to the average modern reader and may be helpful for personal devotional practice. From this type I have selected some for special attention.

The translation which I have consistently used is that of the English version of the Gelineau Psalter. For my own use I have altered some of the language - carefully and respectfully, I hope. I have wanted to liberate the texts from their home territory and bring them into the 21st century. I seldom make an extensive rewrite; I use adaptation which intensifies for me the devotional impact and spiritual witness of these psalms. In particular, I look for language which can reflect my desire to strengthen images and symbols which resonate with the New Story of the cosmos and with the meaning of Sacred Presence in that cosmology.

My background for doing this work has been 'to listen' for years to a small number of psalms each day, in a rotation which uses all 150 of them monthly. That is: I have learned how 'to eaves-drop' on the ancient authors as they are at prayer. I cannot exaggerate the debt I owe to them in assisting my spiritual journey.

I listen to the psalmists from a psychological distance; I do not try to walk in their footsteps. I try to feel and appreciate the deep currents of their faith in, and love for, Yahweh God which permeate all of the psalms and to do this with a minimum of interference from my own cultural and religious bias. However, one major difference between them and us I have been unable to erase: the psalmists' God is conceived as 'out there'. In biblical literature the divine transcendence is emphasized and constantly urged by metaphors of distance from humans, both in temporal space and in the quality of holiness. In the New Story already emerging among us, however, the image of 'Sacred Presence' de-emphasizes divine transcendence in order to acknowledge and rejoice in divine immanence. More is said about this in the last chapter.

The deep devotion of these amazing poets of Yahweh God, these Voices of Faithfulness and Singers of ancient Israel, has been a delight for me to discover. The spiritual intuition and wisdom which they possess have enriched humanity for more than two millennia. However, because we are at a Great Divide in the human spiritual odyssey - with profound changes in how we understand and experience our lives as citizens of the cosmos and in how we image Sacred Presence - it is difficult to know in what way their legacy will contribute to future generations. The few selections presented here set out some of the psalms that I continue to find important, but I am unable to imagine what the entire Book of Psalms will mean to pilgrims of the spirit in the future.

Psalm 19 (abbreviated and adapted)

The cosmos proclaims Sacred Presence
   and the heavens show forth the work of Mystery;
day after day takes up the story
   and night after night makes known the message.

No speech, no word, no voice is heard
   yet their sound goes out through all the Earth,
   their testimony to the utmost bounds of the world.

The cosmos proclaims Sacred Presence
   and the heavens show forth the work of Mystery.

. . . .

The instruction of Yahweh is perfect,
   it revives the soul.
The rule of the Holy One is to be trusted,
   it gives wisdom to those who embrace it.

> The precepts of the Holy One are right,
>   they gladden the heart.
> The command of the Holy One is clear,
>   it gives light to the eyes.
>
> The decrees of the Holy One are truth
>   and all of them just,
> they are more to be desired than gold,
>   than the purest of gold;
> and sweeter are they than honey,
>   than honey from the comb.
> In them your servant finds a Living Word;
>   great reward is in its keeping.
>
> But who can detect all his errors?
> Let hidden faults be known to me that I may repent;
>   keep your servant from presumption of innocence
>   and let it not rule me.
> Then shall I be cleansed from grave sin.
>
> May the spoken words of my mouth,
>   and the unspoken thoughts of my heart,
> win favour in your sight,
>   our Rescuer and our Rock.

Psalm 19 has two distinct sections. The first (much abbreviated here) is a celebration of the cosmos as a revelation of the Divine. There is a 'sound', the Singer declares, that emanates from the universe, a 'Word' that is not like our words but which nevertheless "takes up the story . . . makes known the message". This message is a clarion call to humanity to be amazed at Sacred Presence in the cosmic order, to open ourselves to the Mystery which is the heart of the universe, to yield ourselves in gratitude and awe to the divine Creator.

The second section of this psalm is a celebration of Yahweh's sacred instruction (Torah) to humanity, successively identified as "rule . . . precept . . . command . . . decree". These synonyms give us a sense of why the Singer finds joy in his God: the divine Living Word has the potential to bless and guide him in every circumstance of life. This is the Wisdom which "revives the soul . . . gladdens the heart . . . gives light to the eyes . . . [brings] great reward in its keeping".

Instruction of the soul by the Holy One is seen as another aspect of the same influence of divine Mystery found within the cosmos. Sacred Presence reaches into the human heart both through the wonder and beauty of the surrounding cosmos and through our spiritual openness to a divine Wisdom and Truth within every thing on the Earth, including our own lives. This awareness of the Divine can come to us in reflective silence, or when it breaks in unexpectedly upon us from Nature, or as revealed in the thoughtful words of a friend. The avenues of grace are without number. The psalmist desires these precious intimations of foundational Truth more than he desires "the purest of gold".

"But who can detect all his errors?" Even as our hearts celebrate the generosity of God's Living Word, we can become abruptly aware that our lives do not readily follow the instruction we are receiving. We have "hidden faults", secret sins which when revealed dismay and accuse us. It is easy to slip into "presumption of innocence". With our small religious insights and our little learning about the ways of the Holy One, we slip into the groove of self-satisfaction and lose our way.

The correcting response, however, is immediately at hand:

> "Let hidden faults be known to me that I may repent;
> keep your servant from presumption of innocence
> and let it not rule me.
> Then shall I be cleansed from grave sin."

The closing words remind us of "our Rescuer and our Rock" whose compassionate is endless.

Psalm 32:1-5 (partial and adapted)

Happy the person whose offence is forgiven,
   whose sin is remitted.
O happy the one to whom the Holy One
   imputes no guilt, in whose spirit is no guile.

When I kept my sin secret, my frame was wasted
   and I groaned all the day long.
For night and day your hand was heavy upon me.
   Indeed, my strength was dried up as by the summer's heat.

But now I have acknowledged my sins; my guilt I did not hide.
   I said, "I will confess my offence to the Holy One,"
And You, God, have forgiven the guilt of my sin.

Psalm 51 (partial and adapted)

Response: I rejoice in your compassion, my God,
         in your abundant loving kindness.

Yahweh, my sin is ever before me,
   what is evil in your sight I have done,
   I know that I grieve you.
In your compassion, blot out my offences,
   wash away my guilt
   and cleanse me from my sin.

Response:

You love truth in the heart;
   then in the secret of my heart teach me wisdom.
A pure heart create for me, O God,
   put a steadfast spirit within me.
Do not cast me away from your presence,
   nor deprive me of your Holy Spirit.

Response:

Rescue me, God my helper,
  and my tongue shall speak out your goodness.
O God, open my lips
  and my mouth shall declare your praise;
  a humbled, contrite heart You will not spurn.

Response:

The Christian church, more in the West than in the East, has done the world a serious disservice by harping endlessly upon human sin and the presumed (and vivid) divine punishment for sin. This practice must be rejected as a serious perversion of biblical religion. On the other hand, moral fault and its often disastrous consequences are so evident in society that we would be extremely foolish to ignore this aspect of human nature. The experience of guilt following upon moral fault is a common theme in the Book of Psalms, and this theme is frequently complemented by a call for penitence and proclamation of the divine response of forgiveness. (The liturgical Response given above for Psalm 51 is an example of a common custom: the congregation celebrates the divine compassion and generosity by repeating a central motif of the psalm.)

Emma Herman, in her small book "The Finding of the Cross", makes this observation: "We know from experience how unsanctifying the remembrance of sin can be, and how its alarming echoes may awaken a whole black cavernful of hurtful emotions. We know the impure passion of remorse." Remorse, Herman claims, brings "shame, dejection, weary melancholy and sterile regret", and finally a kind of spiritual paralysis. We become the victims of "outraged self-respect".

Remorse, like healthy repentance, begins in a truthful

recognition of sin; we are disturbed - perhaps shocked - by what we see in our behaviour. But in remorse we make a fundamental mistake. We are looking only at the self and are immobilized and discouraged by what we see. Remorse protests, "Surely I am not that bad?" And when we begin to rationalize our behaviour, "then the last state of that person is worse than the first". Better not to undertake moral self-examination at all than to end up in dishonest self-justification. Remorse humiliates us, but does not take us one step closer to true sorrow (contrition) for sin committed. Herman continues,

> It does not take us long to recognize that the root of our failures in repentance is in self-love. It is our self-pity that breeds that destructive sadness . . . . the fundamental truth is that repentance is not a self-regarding activity; . . . the root of all things good is Mercy . . . penitential sorrow is justified by its threefold fruit of joy, vision and courage.

Herman titles this section of her book, "The Joy of Repentance". This certainly strikes the right chord, because it is truly a joy - a gift of the Sacred - to discover a fault and then begin work to correct it with the strong sense that the Holy One is in the work.

In the early-1960s I was at a large meeting in the Hotel Bessborough in Saskatoon, sitting beside my friend, Diane. She had just returned from visiting a group of young people who were learning the methods of non-violent resistance. One man, who had been assigned the role of passive resister, told her something he had learned. While acting out his assigned role during the week-long exercise, he realized that he was harboring an "internal violence" which quite matched the external violence of his opponents. He discovered that he had a considerable way to go before he would be a non-violent person.

When Diane said those words "internal violence" I felt as though all the bells of the churches in Saskatoon were ringing out! This was true of me. I was so often inwardly angry while working to preserve outward calm. I went home that night and wrote a few words in a small loose-leaf book to name the interior work of transformation for which I need divine help.

In Psalm 32 the Singer says:

> When I kept my sin secret, my frame was wasted
>   and I groaned all the day long. . .
> But now I have acknowledged my sins;
>   my guilt I did not hide.

We can understand only too well why the psalmist celebrates the discovery of sin and welcomes the contrition that will ultimately bring spiritual healing. And then we listen with gratitude to other words in Psalm 51:

> You love truth in the heart;
>   then in the secret of my heart teach me wisdom.
> A pure heart create for me, O God,
>   put a steadfast spirit within me.

These words express so eloquently one of the most important desires that we can name in our spiritual journey. This is the 'truth' that we need for living well, truth which can only come from the heart and has the quality of wisdom. It comes as a gift of the Sacred, little by little, as we find ways deliberately to open ourselves to the Presence.

Psalm 40:1-8   (adapted)

I waited, I waited for Yahweh,
   again and again He stooped to me,
He heard my longing cry.

He drew me from the deadly pit,
   from the miry clay.
He set my feet upon a rock
   and made my footsteps firm.

He put a new song into my mouth,
   praise of our God.
Many shall see and wonder
   and shall trust in Yahweh. . . . . .

How many, my God,
   are the wonders and designs
that You have worked in Creation:
   You have no equal.
Should I proclaim and speak of them
   they are more than I can tell!

Yet, You do not ask for sacrifice and offerings,
   but an open heart.
You do not ask for sacred fire and victim;
   instead, here am I.

In the scroll of the book it stands written
   that I should do your will.
My God, I delight in your instruction
   in the depths of my heart,
   I delight to do your will.

The first three verses share with us the gratitude felt by the Singer who has come through a personal struggle to a renewed sense of the worthwhileness in life. Her/his longing cry had been met by the strengthening gifts of Yahweh; the deadly pit and the miry clay had been exchanged for a rock on which to place firm footsteps into the future. The images employed are deliberately open and undefined. When we fall into our own deadly pits and stumble in our own miry clay, the singer encourages us to discover within ourselves, and give voice to, a sincere longing cry.

The opening words, however, "I waited, I waited", tell us that this Singer did not yet realize (as did some of his people) that Yahweh is always present to us. Unlike the singer of Psalm 139 (see below), this Singer shared the ancient belief that the gods must be summoned or bribed to be present, that Yahweh must be made aware of his people's needs. For this psalmist, the Lord God is the absent Holy One who must be summoned. His/her God is not Sacred Presence who constantly presses upon humanity to be known, who anticipates human need and who in loving kindness waits and desires to feed our spiritual hunger in response to articulated needs. Indeed, faith teaches us that the Holy One does not require to be summoned to our side; it is we who must wake up to the outrageous Loving which constantly besieges us. And then we learn to state our needs in ways which open us to this Loving.

This revolution in spiritual understanding is urgently needed in our own time if we are to advance beyond the customary practices of present world religions and if we are to discover new spiritual foundations for human/Divine communion. (This subject will be considered again in the last chapter.)

The second set of three verses in Psalm 40 tells about a startling truth which had previously been hidden from the Singer. S/he was drawn to the temple through a sense of wonder aroused by the design and beauty of the created world and by faith in Yahweh's care for Israel. S/he went there to participate in ritual acts of the worshipping congregation. But there - in that place and in those rituals - a new word of truth had been revealed: "You do not ask for sacrifice and offerings, but an open heart". The Singer is startled to learn that recitation of the public liturgy can be enriched by an even greater reality, "an open heart". Although the Singer had already learned from the tradition, from "the scroll of the book . . . that I should do your will", now s/he is being called upon to "delight in your instructions in the depths of my heart".

For untold generations this Singer's people had observed the formal public liturgies of the tradition but now a new dimension was being seen. The inward part of the spiritual journey was being glimpsed and celebrated.

A further insight, "You do not ask for sacred fire and victim", would take centuries to become knit into the Hebrew religion. Sacrificial worship in the Jerusalem temple was at the heart of Jewish religion and it remained so until the destruction of the temple by the Romans in 70 CE. What did the Jews do after that catastrophic event, with the central icon of their religion gone? With the birth of Rabbinical Judaism late in the first century the Jews became the 'People of the Book'. The written Torah, and the Oral Torah as sacred commentary upon it, became the new 'temple' of Israel's faith tradition.

Psalm 63   (abbreviated and adapted)

O God, You are my God, for you I long;
   for You my soul is thirsting.
My body pines for You
   like a dry, weary land without water.
So I open myself to You
   and yield to your strength and your glory.

> For your love is better than life,
>   my lips will speak your praise.
> So I will bless You all my life,
>   in your name I will life up my hands.
> My soul shall be filled as with a banquet,
>   my mouth shall praise You.
>
> On my bed I remember You.
>   On You I muse through the night
> for You have been my help;
>   in the shadow of your wings I rejoice.
> My soul clings to You;
>   your right hand holds me fast.

There are times in everyone's life when external circumstances are so overwhelming that one experiences a feeling of utter helplessness. In this situation we are able to appreciate the language of this psalm - a mood and language found in many psalms which are referred to as 'lamentation'. The images of longing, thirsting, and pining - "like a weary land without water" - tell us how desperately this person feels bereft of human help; they are a measure of the Singer's desire to know the presence of the Holy One. S/He cries, "your love is better than life"; and s/he anticipates the time when her/his need will be met,

> "My soul shall be filled as with a banquet,
>   my mouth shall praise you with joy".

Throughout the mystical writings of all religions we encounter depths of desire akin to this. There is a yearning here, arising from realms of soul, that I find contagious. When my own heart is cold and my faith obscured by the shadows of life, I listen to this person's openness to the Divine and I am encouraged. I know that I too can return from spiritual loneliness and darkness, and continue my journey with a good hope.

Psalm 119:33-45   (adapted)

Teach me the Way of your sacred instruction
  and I will follow it to the end of my days.
Train me to observe your law,
  to keep it with my heart.
Guide me in the path of your commands;
  for there is my delight.
Bend my heart to your will
  and not to love of gain.

Keep my eyes from what is false:
  by your Living Word, give me life.
Keep the promise You have made
  to the servant who loves You.
Keep me from the scorn I dread,
  for your decrees are good.

See, I long for your precepts:
  then in your justice, give me life.
Holy One, let your love come upon me,
  the saving help of your promise.
And I shall answer those who taunt me
  for I trust in your word.
Do not take the word of truth from my mouth
  for I trust in your decrees.
I shall always keep your law
  for ever and ever.
I shall walk in the path of freedom
  for I seek your precepts.

Psalm 119, the longest in the Book of Psalms, is in praise of Torah - the divine instruction which ancient Israel learned to place at the heart of her faith. In this psalm selection we find a chorus of synonyms for the enlivening Word of Yahweh: law, commands, will, promise, decrees, precepts. The singer uses this literary device to celebrate the gift s/he values above all else.

Desire for the Living Word is desire for the gift of Sacred Presence experienced as interior truth. There is spiritual instruction we are capable of receiving and accepting for each step in our journey, a Way of Wisdom which is life and joy for us. There is truth for our lives which we urgently need to guide our actions in the immediate future. But, like this Singer, our pursuit of this truth is sometimes misunderstood by others: "Keep me from the scorn I dread . . .and I shall answer those who taunt me."

In a world alienated from the divine Loving, those who desire to know and live by this Loving will be misunderstood - even when the heart of their desire is that the divne blessing may be known throughout the Earth, and for everything and everyone in it.

Psalm 139: 1-14, 23-24   (adapted)

> Holy One, You search me and You know me,
>   You know my resting and my rising,
> You discern my purpose from afar.
>   You mark when I walk or lie down,
>   all my ways lie open to You.
>
> Before ever a word is on my tongue
>   You know it through and through.
> Behind and before You besiege me,
>   your Presence ever near me.
> Too wonderful for me this knowledge,
>   too high, beyond my reach.
>
> O where can I go from your Spirit,
>   or where can I go from your Presence?
> If I climb the heavens, You are there.
>   If I lie in the grave, You are there.
>
> If I take the wings of the dawn
>   and dwell at the sea's furthest end,
> even there You would lead me
>   and You would hold me fast.

> If I say, "Let the darkness hide me
>   and the light around me be night,"
> even darkness is not dark for You
>   and the night as clear as the day.
>
> For it was You who created my being,
>   knit me together in my mother's womb.
> I thank You for the wonder of my being,
>   for the wonders of all your creation.
>
> O search me and know my heart.
>   O test me and know my thoughts.
> See that I follow not the wrong path
>   and lead me in the path of life eternal.

It is not uncommon for people to report a feeling of being pursued by the Divine. Francis Thompson, in his long poem "The Hound of Heaven", captures the heart of this experience:

> I fled him, down the nights and down the days,
> I fled Him, down the arches of the years;
> I fled Him, down the labyrinthine ways
> Of my own mind; and in the mist of tears
> I hid from Him, and under running laughter.

And long centuries earlier, the psalmist sang,

> "Before ever a word is on my tongue
>   You know it through and through.
> Behind and before you besiege me, your Presence ever near me."

In the human Story there is repeated testimony to the experience of divine prevenience (God going before). This is a dramatic awareness that we were known and valued before we believed in our own being and worth. On the other hand, to the human mind so much of our spiritual awakening seems to be the result of personal effort. The mystics, however, are unanimous in telling us that our efforts need to be understood as a response to the preceding divine initiative on our behalf. Who we are becoming, and what we are called to do, are being evoked in us by a Mystery of the divine Loving, by a divine Summons deep within the soul. Our task is to recognize this and respond as best we are able.

This Loving, however, is not an overpowering force of divine predestination. The relationship of the soul to the Holy One is like a dance in which the lead is being given gently and persuasively by Sacred Presence. This One knows us better than we know ourselves. And the wisdom we acquire as we journey is the result of our willing response to the purposes of the Holy One working themselves out in how we think and feel and act.

> O search me and know my heart.
>   O test me and know my thoughts.
> See that I follow not the wrong path
>   and lead me in the path of life eternal.

THE ART OF WOOL-GATHERING

We stand astride one of the great divides in the human odyssey. For us, true religion can no longer be rooted in the ancient arts of courting the divine favour: pleading, interceding, petitioning, and making sacrificial offerings in order to catch the attention of the gods and to win their intervention for our interests. . . We live in a time which is exciting and rewarding, but difficult.
("Sacred Presence")

From time immemorial, humans have offered prayers in order to influence the gods and to gain their favourable actions on our behalf. Even our secularized culture seems to believe that there might be some divine help 'out there' and that it is wise to try to access that help. Children continue to be trained to ask, at bedtime on their knees, for God "to bless Mummy and Daddy, brother and sister". But for many contemporary adults, 'out there' has lost its numinous quality, its special character as the place of the Sacred, and prayers of asking are disappearing from our lives. So I come again to the subject of prayer, to be considered here as an issue in itself, a third and personal "Voice from the Journey".

As one who has conducted uncounted numbers of public ceremonies for Baptism, Marriage and Burial of the Dead, I have been accutely aware that many people have no way to connect with much of the god language being used. This is very sad, because corporate prayer has little depth of meaning if we lack helpful language for speaking about and entering into communion with the Sacred. In the next chapter I discuss in detail present efforts toward a revolution in the language of faith, but here I want to respond to a deeper question. What can we learn about the activity of prayer itself as a means to be open to Sacred Presence?

In my mid teens, when I had mastered the sport of downhill skiing sufficiently to tackle sizeable slopes, on occasional weekends I went north of my home in Montreal to the Laurentian Mountains. Experiencing the beautiful terrain and traversing the slopes with sufficient speed to enjoy the wind whistling past me, I often found myself singing aloud. It was a kind of ecstasy. It was spontaneous, joyful and appropriate. It was a way of prayerfulness. I would say now that it was a gift of deep connection between the Sacred within the natural world and within my own body/mind/soul. I was celebrating the interface between the material order, myself, and the Sacred. Skiing had become a spiritual experience.

As I sang my heart out on the ski slopes, I was not aware of experiencing a challenge to traditional patterns of religious faith in which I had been nurtured. On the contrary, they were being tapped for a new experience of interior life the extent of which I could not have imagined at that time. Although I did not know it then, the adventure of prayer lay not far ahead.

In 1950, I joined a religious society where I was required to follow a Rule of Life. One requirement was to say daily morning and evening prayers. I had never before accepted such a discipline, so to help myself I searched carefully in a small book of prayers and found a suitable one to use each morning. Unfortunately, I never got up in time to say this prayer before having to rush off to work. However, during the long ride on bus and streetcar to my place of employment, while standing in the midst of crowded, swaying bodies I recited my prayer several times, five mornings each week. It was not easy to be attentive to what I was saying but I persisted. Later I found and memorized another prayer and this I said at other times of most days. Saying these two prayers 'worked' - maybe not with God but certainly for me. I was learning about the act of praying.

I find it helpful to distinguish between prayers and prayer. 'Prayers' refers to words we say or sing, but 'prayer' moves in the heart. Prayer happens when soul is present to the Sacred. Rabbi Abraham Heschel says that "prayer is a capacity to face the sacred moment." All religious traditions understand this distinction and in their best moments they encourage the saying of prayers as a means of entering into prayer. In what follows here, I find it helpful to speak in terms of the practice of 'reflection' as leading to a 'state of prayer'.

Earlier, when discussing the spiritual journey, I described one practice of reflection which uses the exercise of "Seek, Wait, See". Now I want to describe another approach to reflection which provides a complement to that exercise.

Monica Furlong was well-known in the latter part of the twentieth century as an English writer on the spiritual life. In one of her smaller books she proposed "wool-gathering" as a good approach to the mystery of prayer. Wool-gathering, she suggested, is a kind of free-wheeling and exploratory thinking. It is thinking that is allowed to wander, to be unfocussed. It is as though a central part of the mind watches another part of the mind meandering here and there, as it brings to our attention different parts of the world. Wool-gathering results in a collection of apparently random thoughts as they are slowly being gathered into the stillness of our quiet time. Ideas, people, enthusiasms, painful experiences, struggles, fears and hopes - all these and more are allowed to surface in the mind. Anything can be included in wool-gathering.

Through this kind of uncontrolled mental spiralling certain things are allowed to come to the Centre of ourselves as subjects for focussed reflection. This is a useful way to discover what needs our attention as we are still and quiet. This practice is also a very effective way to deal with 'distractions' - the most frequently named bugbear of people who are learning to pray. Monica Furlong might be heard to say, "Take this foe called distraction and make it into a helpmate. Make allies of the distracted thoughts which are disturbing you and discover which of them you must deliberately hold now, in this time apart, within your interior watching and caring. Find the most urgent thoughts and feelings which are demanding and needing your loving attention now."

Wool-gathering promotes the unpredictable; in its way it becomes an art form. It responds beautifully to the truth in the words of the Gospel of John: "The wind blows where it chooses, and you hear the sound of it, but you do not know where it comes from or where it goes. So it is with everyone who is born of the Spirit." Within the randomness of wool-gathering we can learn to allow the Spirit to show us which parts of our world need our prayerful attention now.

The practice of wool-gathering entered my quiet times several years after I had developed a firm daily discipline of 'saying prayers'. Alongside the structured prayers I now placed a time for unstructured thought. Sometime later, twenty years into wool-gathering and looking back, I discovered that I had slowly been making a significant shift in what I was doing. I was no longer using prayers to gain some kind of divine intervention or influence in our world; instead, I was learning to hold myself and other parts of the world in love, in the Presence. I was no longer 'saying prayers' to a God out there. My soul work was becoming a means of searching out the spiritual depths of whatever concerned me most in the daily round: my own life (work, struggles, pain, desires, ideas), family and friends, my community, the struggles of humanity for justice and peace, and so much more. In this way I was also gaining a deeper sense of the Sacred in whose Presence and by whose grace I was making these soul connections with my world.

Looking back over those years I discovered that 'saying prayers' had gradually changed. I had learned how to be present 'with intention and attention'; I had learned to pray. I learned how to be present to the Sacred, taking care to bring into these times many different pieces of my world. I learned to ponder what occupied my thoughts, to be grateful, to yearn, or to lament. This may be close to what Buddhists refer to as 'mindfulness'.

Sometimes I wrote down what I felt and thought, and this developed new words, a new language. This new language entered into the accumulating written text of my journal and helped to shape the texture of my spiritual journey. As with so many other people, keeping a written journal had become for me a valuable practice.

An essential element in this transition from saying prayers to the work of prayer is to leave behind all language about an interventionist deity. There is no god out there waiting to receive prayers and hymns. *But there is Sacred Presence in our midst -* pressing within and around us to enable new wisdom and new life in the believing community. And just as we can help ourselves in our personal times to move from saying prayers to the work of prayer, the pilgrim community can learn to make the same transition. Our changing and deepening awareness of Sacred Presence can become reflected in new and different liturgical language, music, song, drama and body movement. We need to experiment. Many of our public liturgical forms can be reshaped to point eloquently to the Sacred as immanent, as immediate. And then the quality of our shared times of prayer deepens.

For one thing, we may become more aware that our public liturgical celebrations are actually times of 'sacred recital' for the purpose of helping us to re-engage with our communal Story. We discover that this sacred recital is a valuable means by which we teach ourselves about who we are as a community of faith. And, it seems evident to me, we also become more open to Sacred Presence who uses our liturgy to instruct and renew the present life of the believing community.

Just as there is a communal faith Story which shapes and expresses the life of the believing community, so also each of us has a personal Story which tells who we are. And just as there is the community's shared liturgy to express its Story, so we can create a 'mini liturgy' by which we regularly recall our personal Story. Praying a personal liturgy enables us to recall where and how we began our journey, how we have continued it and have sometimes forgotten it, and where we are in the journey now. We can learn to recognize and record how we have been guided and strengthened, and to describe what are the characteristic ways in which we have failed and then been able to resume our path. All these different aspects of our personal journeying reveal our Story.

The contents of our personal Story are gathered over time into a variety of sources. Poems, quotations from letters and books, reflections we have written for ourselves, aphorisms which capture something of the Sacred Wisdom speaking within us - all these highlight the Story of who we are.

The thanksgivings, reflections and aspirations set out below are the result of soul work using both the structured form of

"Seek, Wait, See" and the unstructured, gentle art of wool-gathering. Each text has a considerable history of formation. Each is the fruit of a process of trial and error which gradually uncovers the right words in which to express my feelings and thoughts. I seek patiently over months (sometimes years) in an attempt to find this or that word or phrase which can better express what I am feeling and thinking. Each of these is a work in progress. "It is in the struggle to articulate truthfully that our words become capable of actually communicating truth".

These are not model reflections; they are the results of the kind of soul work which I have found it worthwhile to do in the spiritual journey. It is the process, not the products, that I seek to recommend.

Wool-gathering and structured prayer both move us to focussed listening at the 'still point'. And sometimes the external world unexpectedly intrudes itself sharply and clearly with its own Voice; to listen to this is also soul work. In sum: we listen in the depths of our being for whatever the Spirit is teaching, and then seek the thoughts and language to express it to our self as truthfully as we can.

>Sacred Presence
>Ground of Being
>Wellspring of Truth and Love
>
>You are hidden and disclosed
>>in the unfolding patterns and powers of the Universe
>>in the beauty and rhythms of planet Earth
>>and in each creature's struggle to fulfil its purpose
>
>You are hidden and disclosed
>>in gracious words and deeds of people
>>in lives of prophets and sages
>>and in Jesus of Nazareth

      and as a strange, unbidden quickening
      within humans hearts
           You are hidden and disclosed

These words are an attempt to open myself to the Mystery of the divine Other. But I do not address a discreet, Almighty Being. Rather, I desire to yield myself to the infinite and sustaining embrace of Sacred Presence who flows in and through all created being. The degree to which these words actually accomplish a specific intention varies from time to time but they always allow me to express my continual wish to be open to the most important Gift that humans can desire.

    Of the Essence of this divine Reality I know nothing. But I believe there is a Great Loving who desires to enter into communion with the mystery within each and every creature. My words, therefore, are not magical incantation; they are a way of naming the Reality which I believe underlies the whole created order and a practice which helps me to be still and to be present.

    In our quiet times of prayer, with attention and consent, we seek to be open to the invitation 'to be present'; to be here, to be now. Reflection is a medium for soul work.

      Holy One - Holy and Gracious
      Eternal Wisdom, Nurturing Spirit
      You surround us, You indwell us
      You call our hearts
         to a communion of love
           with Earth and all her creatures
      You draw us in love to yourself
      You teach our hearts to sing

Over time, each person discovers her or his own language by which to name and be open to Sacred Presence. The personal lexicon which each of us develops in our reflections is one of the important ways we have of tutoring the spiritual life.

> Life-Giver:
> may this day be a time of grace,
> my heart open to the Truth and Beauty
>   of Earth and all her creatures.
>
> Light within:
> teach me to respond to your Presence,
>   your Generosity, and your Living Word
> with trust, gratitude and joy.
>
> Nurturing Spirit:
> help me to live easily
> in lowliness and service
> gentle in thought, word and deed
> that from this small life
>   - wounded and healed, broken and restored -
> may come works of love.

"Do you not know that you are God's temple and that God's Spirit dwells in you?" (1 Cor 3:16). Paul the Apostle urges us to understand that the indwelling Presence, the divine Generosity, and the Living Word are gifts for us to treasure and explore.

From my mid teens onwards, the person of Jesus of Nazareth has remained central to my journey. During each phase of my changing discipleship I have discovered new language by which to be present to him.

The words of this reflection took about ten years to reach their present form, and I have no way of knowing if they will be changed again. They help me to be present to Jesus of Nazareth in a manner which honours who he is for me now. There are important reminders in this reflection of what I have come to imagine about him through reading the Gospels, and of what I have come to believe about him through my life experience.

> Jesus of Nazareth, Master,
> > prophet in Galilee of old,
> radiant with the Mystery of Lowliness,
> you were a servant of your people,
> you taught and lived the Reign of God.
>
> Though powerful enemies
> > rejected your message
> > and broke your body,
> Holy Love in you prevailed.
> > Your Truth and Love abide among us.
>
> Beloved Teacher and Friend:
> > I desire to live this day as one of your disciples,
> > to be open to Gifts of the Spirit
> > which come to those who follow your Way;
> that learning compassion, justice and peace
> > we may help to heal Earth and her People.

From the psalmists, the Singers of ancient Israel, I learned that being in the Presence of Yahweh sometimes brought them sacred instruction, 'Oral Torah'. In the text of a psalm and with no prior explanation, the reader suddenly finds her/himself faced with words which the faithful Singer has 'heard', received and recorded as a gift from Yahweh.

I too, occasionally, find words of instruction being given. And for them I use the preface, 'out of the Depths, Spirit speaks'. During one such time I learned to value the word 'Gift', and to understand how central to the journey is our ability to receive what is being offered by the divine Generosity. Being able to receive is itself an important gift of Sacred Presence.

> out of the Depths, Spirit speaks:
>
> All is Gift.
>   Receive what you need with gratitude,
>   give to others needs with generosity,
> and be grateful for all that is provided for this day.
>
>   When you share in my loving
>   I take you into my grieving;
>   When you share in my grieving
>   I take you deeper into my loving;
>   So that in both
>   you may know Me
>   and enter into my Joy.

Israel's greatest prophets sometimes spoke of Yahweh's 'grief', which they understood as a response to Israel's ingratitude and faithlessness. Jesus, too, grieved in his heart for his contemporaries' lack of faithfulness. Many other people have also learned to 'grieve God's grief' as a consequence of participating in the divine Loving. And together these lead to something deeper still: the Mystery of the divine Joy.

out of the Depths, Spirit speaks:

> The Way of the Spirit
> is generous loving and doing justice
>   among family and friends
>   in community and nation
>   and in solidarity with compassionate people everywhere

'The Way of the Spirit' is a central mark of truthful living and those who respond with an open heart becomes friends of the Holy One. And this Way is not fixed nor pre-determined; it emerges within us as we ourselves grow spiritually.

When Spirit speaks, sometimes responding words form in us and soul responds,

> Holy One, make me one of your friends:
>   the merciful, the peacemakers, the truthtellers
>   those who hunger and thirst for the right
>   who take risks in seeking justice for themselves
>   and for others
>   who sustain your 'little ones' in times of peril

In Matthew's gospel 3:3-14, sometimes called the Sermon on the Mount, Jesus identified basic guidelines for friendship with the Holy One. To these names I add 'truthtellers'. Deliberate falsehoods are commonplace among us in public discourse and truthtelling is much needed today for society's well-being.

I also add, "those who take risks .... who sustain ...."
Courage to resist injustice is in high demand these days when deliberate injustice is common. Active compassion is essential when there are so many little ones who become so-called 'collateral victims' of violence in the world.

Cosmic inter-connectedness is demonstrated by the sciences of physics, mathematics and biology, and is taught in Aboriginal spirituality. One of my images for the interdependence of everything is the 'Cosmic Web'. In my imagination, each created being - past, present and future - is a point of light within the Cosmic Web and the unity among us is the Radiant Loving of the Divine.

> My soul, seek to be poor in spirit:
>   be still
>   be naked
>   be attentive
> a single point of light in the Cosmic Web
> where All are gathered to the Sacred
>   where each one learns their Name

The spiritual journey is an adventure. We learn to expect and to welcome new insights, new invitations, new pathways.

> Holy Wisdom,
>   divine Companion
>   Light upon the Way:
> in our beginnings you call us into a journey
>   each day you call us into
>   new Truth, new Goodness, new Loving.
>
> My soul,
>   be present to the Holy One;
>   at the Still Point listen
>   with attention and consent .....

> Embrace of the divine Yearning
> > draw me to yourself
>
> Fire of the divine Loving
> > purify me in thought, word and deed
>
> Light of the divine Wisdom
> > guide me into my Truth
>
> Mystery of divine Being
> > > hidden and disclosed
> > let me lose myself
> > and find myself
> > in You

Yearning, Loving, Wisdom, Being ..... each of these words images an activity of Sacred Presence, each of them is a soul experience that we cannot find nor initiate ourselves. By naming them we seek to open ourselves to these wondrous Gifts.

Sacred Presence, You are hidden from us,

> *but You give yourself to us in overwhelming generosity.*

You break open our hearts with the floodtide of your loving

> *You inflame our minds with the wonder of your speaking*

You bind up our soul wounds with your gentle compassion

> *You gird our wills with the strength of your Spirit*

And you give us pilgrim friends with whom to share the journey.

> *From dawn to dark, in joy and thanksgiving*
>
> *we celebrate your Presence in our lives,*
>
> *our lives in your Presence.*

Questions for Discussion

What are some of your personal experiences of Earth as sacred? If you have favourite narrative books or poetry about Earth, you might like to share readings from them with your group.

To which of the poems in this section do you respond positively? or not at all? why?

What difference does it make to how we live when we see Earth as sacred?

....

To which of these Psalm Singers do you respond most positively? Why?

There is a sense of urgency in many of the psalms. Sometimes this comes from the presence of external forces, sometimes from within the Singer. Reflecting on these psalm selections, how would you describe the urgency being experienced by each Singer?

....

To what extent have you, in the past or present, found yourself unable to pray as your heart seems to desire? What have you learned about the nature of your difficulties? What have you done to move beyond them?

There are many creative ways to do 'woolgathering'. What experience have you had of this work?

If you belong to a congregation, what have you found assists the community to pray, rather than simply to say prayers? What inhibits the spiritual work of corporate prayer? What changes in public liturgy would you encourage and support?

THE COSMOS, THE SACRED and a NEW STORY

Humans need stories - grand, compelling stories - that help to orient us in our lives and in the cosmos. The Epic of Evolution is such a story, beautifully suited to anchor our search for planetary consensus, telling us of our nature, our place, our context.
   (Ursula Goodenough, "Sacred Depths of Nature")

The cosmological narrative is the primary narrative of any people, for this is the story that gives to a people their sense of the universe. It explains how things came to be in the beginning and how they came to be the way they are. . . It is a healing story, a power story, a guiding story. All human roles are continuations, further elaborations, expansions, and fulfillments of this story. So any creative deed at the human level is a continuation of the creativity of the universe.
   (Thomas Berry, "Evening Thoughts")

The Mystery of Sacred Presence within the cosmos is somewhat analogous to the mystery of soul within the human frame. Just as soul is the interior reality of our body/mind, the Sacred is believed to be the interior Reality of the cosmos. I have already invited you to ponder with me the wonder of soul. Now I invite you to consider some aspects of the universal Mystery of the Sacred.

In this final chapter I recall the long history of how humanity has expressed its awareness of the Sacred. I discuss our contemporary understanding of how Earth exists within an enormous and expanding cosmos and how this vision has given birth to a search for a new Story of the meaning of human life. And I probe some of the implications of our new awareness of Sacred Presence for the transformation of humanity's historic religions.

A new cosmology and a new spirituality provide the context for the Sacred Journey that is the subject of this book.

TRADITIONAL SYMBOLISM OF THE SACRED

Theology - wisdom about the Sacred - is a human endeavour. As children we may have learned that "God made us". But it is more accurate to say that humans have always been making images both material and mental of gods, and have constantly fashioned architecture, ritual, music and language to connect themselves with those gods. Because we are by nature spiritual, it is not surprising that we have searched the heavens and Earth for signs of a spiritual Presence who is our Companion in life's journey. It is this search that has resulted in a long and complex series of stories in each of which the Sacred is presented as a vital part of the human journey.

At first there seems to have been a generalized human sense of the Sacred as embedded throughout the natural world, expressed in the scholarly term 'animism'. Early people believed the entire world was permeated by Spirit and that each creature was in its own manner an expression of the Sacred. Later, humans projected their sense of the Sacred upon specially chosen subjects: they populated their world with mythological figures such as sacred animals, fish and birds, sacred trees and mountains. Later still, human forms were used to represent divine and semi-divine beings.

In the small and widely scattered human groups of palaeolithic times, perhaps as long ago as 50,000 years, significant experiences of the Sacred were being shared among group members. This sharing fostered communal religious institutions within which spiritual traditions could be articulated and consolidated. Because of the continuity of these endeavours in a multitude of places and over many thousands of years, each succeeding generation of humans found vital cultural practices already present in their community, nurturing local traditions of their life with the Sacred. Each such tradition during its lifetime became a self-perpetuating context within which a continuing sense of the Sacred was articulated, formalized and enriched. And within later neolithic times, say from 12,000 to 3,000 BCE, extravagent public buildings and ceremonies to celebrate the Sacred were among the most important artifacts of social life.

In this long process of changing symbolization of the Sacred, all the images had terrestrial origins. That is, the images and symbolic acts were drawn from people's experience of Earth and from an awed awareness of the heavens. By myth and symbol, by image, metaphor and story, humans cast the Sacred within familiar forms. People structured their sacred stories around imagined fabulous events and personages which were idealized projections of their daily experience. Heavenly realities have in fact been wondrously transformed replicas of earthly realities, even within the most sophisticated world religions of recent millenia.

This process of symbolizing the human sense of the Sacred within specially chosen familiar forms has been normative for tens of thousands of years. And all this spiritual endeavour presumed a cosmology in which Earth was a fixed centre around which the sun and moon circled and stars looked down. For increasing numbers of people today, however, both this cosmology and the varied religious expressions belonging to it are proving to be much too small and much too materialistic. Living within these classical cosmic stories we feel spiritually under-nourished.

A NEW COSMOLOGY

The great new fact of the human spiritual journey is that all previous cosmologies together with the religious imagery and ritual which emerged within them are rapidly becoming obsolete. We know now that humans inhabit a tiny planet within a very small solar system of a regional galaxy, all of which are parts of an unimaginably large and expanding universe. Religious language and liturgy, interior reflection and spiritual searching, now find themselves challenged to understand, articulate and celebrate a sense of Sacred Presence embedded within this fascinating cosmos.

In 1968, when from their circling spaceship astronauts transmitted to Earth pictures of a beautiful, blue-green Earth floating in space, the human religious enterprise was forever transformed. A desire to be open to Sacred Presence must now express itself within our knowledge of the deep space/time of an expanding universe. This knowledge complements other knowledge of the exquisite molecular structure of Earth's smallest life-forms. Both macrocosm and microcosm astonish us. This new perspective constitutes an exciting invitation to engage actively in discovering a New Story within which the human spiritual adventure can continue.

Henceforth, how we speak about the Sacred must engage with this new cosmology. Only with great care can the Sacred be usefully referred to as 'father', 'shepherd', 'teacher', or in other substantive personal nouns. Personal nouns and pronouns risk falsely humanizing the essence of the Sacred. For example, our customary use of religious language fails - one might say especially fails - in the common term 'Creator'. This word carries the sense of a force extrinsic to the material order that is outside and acting upon the universe. But everything science tells us about the evolution of the cosmos urges us to wonder about a creative Sacred Presence which actively permeates and is intrinsic to the entire cosmos of space/time, a Mystery of divine creativity within the material order.

In contrast to problems with personal nouns and pronouns, however, spiritual discourse might well continue to use familiar verb forms to describe divine activity in Earth. These include speaking, teaching, blessing, correcting, guiding, embracing. Such verbs point by analogy to *how we experience the effects of the Sacred in our lives*. Active verbs allow us to express an awareness of Sacred Presence engaging us. But there is a radical difference between traditional use of these verbs and a use embedded in the new cosmology. The difference may be expressed as a question: How do we imagine the Sacred in Its relationship to the material order? Is the Sacred extrinsic or intrinsic?

World religions today face a challenge never before experienced in the human spiritual journey. Previously the symbolism, language and liturgies of faith have functioned comfortably within symbolic use of prominent features of temporal and spacial realms. Through superb works of the visual and plastic arts, in beautiful music and graceful architecture, human imagination has crafted from Earth and the heavens a religious environment where faith can be quickened and flourish. But - and this has been a fatal flaw - even the best of this work has failed to guide us into a healthy relationship with our fundamental home, Earth. During the past few millenia dominant traditions of the world religions have explicitly denigrated the 'base nature of matter' and affirmed the 'spiritual goal of heavenly life'. Even Christian sacramentalism elevates the spiritual which is being signified well above the material which is the signifier. For the most part, religion has treated Earth as an object available for human needs and wants. The cost of this tragic error is now being paid by Earth herself and all her creatures.

If our present search to respond creatively to cosmic Sacred Presence is to be explored and mobilized, we need a New Story in which Earth herself is affirmed as sacred.

IMMANENCE AND TRANSCENDENCE

> Primitive man, grossly superstitious though he may be, is also scientist and technologist. . . He accepted a world of reality, a natural, everyday, observable world in which he existed, and whose forces he utilized in order to survive. The other aspect of his mind, the mystical part seeking answers to questions, clothed the visible world in a shimmering haze of magic.
> (Loren Eiseley, "The Firmament of Time")

Our distant ancestors felt that there were fearsome and mysterious powers in the natural environment which controlled their lives. For them, the Sacred was entirely immanent, saturating the world, embedded in everything. The daily rising and setting of the sun; the twenty-eight day cycle of the moon; unpredictable and violent storms, floods and droughts; the presence around them of a host of other sentient beings . . . . so much in the natural environment seemed to them to possess a mysterious force which was radically different from themselves but which also daily engaged them. As they became more mentally acute and more subtle in enquiry, they visualized 'spirit powers' present in every familiar terrestrial form, both animate and inanimate. Some powers were thought to be malevolent and others beneficent; and all of these were invested with supernatural reality which was to be approached cautiously and with reverence through appropriate rituals. The Sacred was immanent. Immanence has the dictionary meaning of "naturally present, inherent; permanently pervading the universe".

In those times of early human culture, a 'sympathetic magic' developed which allowed people to be safely present to this mysterious and sometimes overpowering spiritual reality. A class of specially trained and gifted persons (shamans, witch doctors, priests and priestesses, wise women and wise men) mediated between humans and the powers. And with continuing social evolution the powers became personified as discreet 'gods', possessing forms at first animal and later human. The practice of magic yielded to the practice of religion.

In scholarly literature dealing with magic and religion, the generalized term 'sacred' is frequently used to identify the encompassing power which people felt to be present around them. For example, Mother Goddess rites of fertility were strong affirmations of the Sacred as immanent. Fertility in nature and in people was experienced as a manifestation of sacred power which bestows upon living forms the possibility of continuity through death into new life. Humans lived with a profound respect for Earth and its generous provision for life, and this fostered close attention to and partnership with the seasons and forces of Nature.

In most parts of the Christian world during the last 2000 years, however, the immanence of the Divine has become increasingly lost from our awareness. This has been due in part to an emphasis in late Hebrew Tradition on Yahweh God as 'transcendent'. This term means 'over against', 'other than', and contrasts with immanent. For the Hebrews of the few hundred years before the time of Jesus of Nazareth, Yahweh was distinguished from the gods of neighbouring peoples by virtue of his separation in Holiness and transcendent Majesty. This emphasis passed into Christian theology - with a consequent stress on the separation of the eternal God from a temporal, dependent and transient material creation which He [*sic*] had made.

What received less comment from Christians, however, was that this separation of the Holy One from the material creation resulted in matter being de-sacralized. This sacred/secular split resulted in people seeing Earth as an object for domination and exploitation.

The loss in Christian teaching of a sense of the Divine as immanent within the created order was amplified by strong currents of thought coming from the culture of ancient Greece. Both the elevation of human reason in Greek philosophy and a keen interest in detailed analysis of the natural order advanced the process of de-sacralizing Earth. This was a world view which ultimately banished the Sacred to the realms of a remote Unmoved Mover. Thus, from both Hebrew/Christian and Greek influences, the God of the European peoples became an external Presence and Power separated from a material order no longer viewed as sacred and now open to unrestrained human exploitation. This religious/cultural inheritance has prevailed up to present times.

During the last couple of centuries two powerful winds of change have emerged which carry the possibility of reversing this collective loss of awareness of the Divine as immanent. The first is the new cosmology already referred to. In response to this development, a new wave of Christian thought has emerged. A prime example is Pierre Teilard de Chardin who was an eminent Christian palaeontologist living in the late 19th to mid 20th centuries. He proposed that the universe was generated and has been sustained from its beginning by a 'within', by a thrust of sacred Being immanent within the unfolding processes of the natural order.

Many thinkers have built on the work of de Chardin, among whom is eco-theologian Thomas Berry. In one of his books he writes,

> We bear the universe in our being as the universe bears us in its being. The two have a total presence to each other and to that deeper mystery out of which both the universe and ourselves have emerged.
> ("The Dream of the Earth", 1998)

Both of these men, as well as many other writers, understand "that deeper mystery" to be the same Reality which countless previous generations of humans venerated as the Sacred. That is, the Sacred is being seen again as immanent within the natural order. Divine immanence is being affirmed as the dynamic Presence inherent in the evolution of the universe as its Ground of Being. In this view, the Sacred is 'present within' everything.

The second wind of change which challenges our collective loss of a sense of the Divine as immanent within the material order is a growing interest in personal religious experience. This wind of change came to the attention of many people with the publication in 1902 of William James' book, "The Varieties of Religious Experience". Within the new discipline of psychology, human religious experience began to be examined in terms of the dynamics of the human psyche. In this work, the Sacred is understood as 'present to' as well as 'present within' humanity in its various stages of development, a point discussed at some length in the second chapter of this book. It seems apparent that we cannot banish the Sacred from human experience any more than we can banish the Sacred from Earth and the cosmos. In the future, all human spirituality will include strong affirmation of the immanent Sacred both as 'present within' the entire created order and as 'present to' the human soul.

What can be said, then, about divine transcendence which for centuries has been prominent in much religious teaching? In the past, transcendence has been strongly associated with a supernatural revelation of the divine will and purpose for creation and with revealed moral standards to guide human behaviour. Deviation from these standards were believed to bring divine punishment. But this extrinsic divinity, speaking 'from above' and into the creation, is an image of the Divine that now needs to be questioned. As we think our way into implications of the new cosmology, divine transcendence will be understood in another way.

Morality in Western society today is becoming more 'natural' and less 'supernatural', more drawn from daily experience and less regarded as revealed by a timeless god. People commonly emphasize, for example, the virtues of honesty, truthfulness, empathy and compassion without reference to divinity. We urge attention to the Golden Rule in its original Confucian form, "Do no evil to others that you do not wish to have done to yourself", which comes from 400 years before the time of Jesus of Nazareth. And we are being forced by events around us to notice that Nature herself is bringing moral judgment on patterns of human abuse of the natural order. The evidence of climate change, extensive loss of irreplacable topsoil, the near-elimination of major fish stocks, continuing destruction of critical forest cover, the loss of thousands of species of life due to loss of habitat resulting from human actions . . . human immorality is being exposed and condemned for its obvious stupidity and fatal consequences. Both ethics and moral standards emerge from our relationship with Earth.

An example of morality as natural rather then supernatural is described eloquently in these words of Ronald Wright (quoted in the magazine, *Walrus*).

> Our greatest experiment - civilization itself - will succeed only if it can live on nature's terms, not man's. To do this we must adopt principles in which the short term is trumped by the long; in which caution prevails over ingenuity; in which the absurd myth of endless growth is replaced by respect for natural limits; in which progress is steered by precautionary wisdom.

For some 2500 years in the West, belief in divine transcendence was used to support obedience to a presumed revealed divine moral will and purpose. This belief sought to give not only precise content but also effective motivation for the good life, to supply not only the subject matter of good living but also the intention to follow through in action. Today however many thoughtful people look into the natural order and the intricacies of its living systems to discern the content of ethical wisdom and moral standards. In this discernment they are moderately successful. But society is far less successful in meeting the challenge to live this vision and to practise its morality. For this we need soul resources found in sound spiritual practice supported by the discipline of an intentional spiritual journey.

As for the continuing significance of divine transcendence, for this we must look elsewhere.

THE DIVINE INITIATIVE

Awareness of the Divine as both immanent and transcendent finds support in a central aspect of biblical teaching which has been called 'the divine intiative'. Foundational stories of both Hebrew and Christian traditions affirm that the human search to know the Holy One is constantly preceded and stimulated by the search of the Holy One for us. Before we desire to know Sacred Presence, Sacred Presence is seeking to reveal Itself to us (unfortunately in our language there is no pronoun adequate to refer to ultimate Mystery as personal).

The heart of the divine initiative is manifested as a Loving Presence which is self-limiting. That is, the divine loving never forces its way into the human heart. As a constant, hidden and yearning Presence, it is forever calling to the beloved to know and welcome it. The Hebrew-Christian tradition teaches that hidden Sacred Presence is revealed to humans through acts of self-disclosure which are recognized by us in proportion to our readiness for that disclosure.

This teaching is central to the Christian spiritual path. It found expression, for example, in the mystical tradition of 16th century Spain:

> Teresa and John speak [in symbolic language] of 'finding' God and of 'growing into union' with God. [But] they do not believe this is something that can really be achieved, for the simple reason that union with God already exists. Everyone always has been and always will be in union with God. This union is so deep and complete that seeking God must include self-knowledge, and self-knowledge must include the search for God. Teresa heard God's voice in prayer saying, "Seek yourself in Me, and in yourself seek Me." . . . The problem for most of us is that we don't realize how united we are with God.

(Gerald May, "The Dark Night of the Soul")

In the biblical documents, as well as in the testimony throughout history of countless pilgrims of the spiritual life, the Holy One is known as both hidden and disclosed. Yahweh God is known to Israel through 'theophanies' ('theos', god; 'phanos', manifest). Yahweh self-manifests to Israel as and when Yahweh determines; otherwise he remains the Hidden God. The storytellers of ancient Israel treasured and repeated traditional tales of the self-disclosing God until eventually these stories found their way into the written sacred text. Major theophanies are recorded in the Hebrew Scriptures as experienced by Abraham, Moses, Elijah, Isaiah, Ezekiel - to mention only some of the most dramatic. (Sadly, biblical writers were not much interested in the spiritual experiences of women.)

On the other hand, the Hebrew Scriptures also record the nation's constant 'forgetting' of their God. Yahweh is not only the self-disclosing God; he is also hidden from the people because they do not live in ways which allow or encourage them to be open to Yahweh. For Israel, the mystery of Sacred Presence is found in this alternation between divine hiddenness and divine self-disclosure.

The same was true in the early Christian church. For the first Christians, Jesus was the ultimate theophany. They believed that in the humanity of Jesus they were seeing the Hidden God come among them in self-disclosure. Or to say this in a different way: the Hidden God takes the initiative in Jesus of Nazareth to disclose to the world a profound revelation of Sacred Presence. But even this astonishing disclosure becomes clouded for faithful Christian believers who regularly find themselves 'waiting upon God' in the darkness of faith. Christian believers have always had to learn to be present to the Hidden God by faith, hope and love.

Our experience of divine self-disclosure can be said to point to the 'immanence' of the Sacred. Our experience of the divine hiddenness can be said to point to the 'transcendence' of the Sacred. And in terms of daily human experience, the divine transcendence is more apparent than is the divine immanence.

RELIGIONLESS CHRISTIANITY

> We are proceeding towards a time of no religion at all: men [sic] as they are now simply cannot be religious any more. . . Our whole nineteen-hundred-year-old Christian preaching and theology rests upon the "religious premise" of man . . . But if one day it becomes apparent that this *a priori* "premise" simply does not exist, but was a historical and temporary form of human self-expression, i.e. if we reach the stage of being radically without religion - what does that mean for Christianity?
> It means that the linchpin is removed from the whole structure of our Christianity to date.
> (Dietrich Bonhoeffer: "Letters and Papers from Prison")

Dietrich Bonhoeffer was a significant theologian of the Church in Germany from the mid 1920's to 1945 when he was executed for presumed association with a plot to assassinate Hitler. During the two years in prison he wrote to friends some of his reflections on the future of the Christian Church, and since the 1960s these letters and papers have become a source of much interest, speculation and controversy. He is the author of the often-quoted phrases, "religionless Christianity" and "man come of age". He suggested that the present time is ripe for a radical revision of Christian teaching, as for example in the following quotations: "Man has learned to cope with all questions of importance without recourse to God as a working hypothesis";

"We should find God in what we do know, not in what we don't; not in outstanding problems, but in those we have already solved"; and "It is not some religious act which makes a Christian what he is, but participation in the suffering of God in the life of the world".

To my knowledge, no one has been able to plumb adequately the complex depths of Bonhoeffer's searching comments and questions, but many people have found his thoughts profoundly stimulating. For myself, one result of pondering the possible meaning of a "religionless Christianity" is to locate the roots of Christian moral insight and endeavour within our life on Earth - as an aspect of human experience - and no longer to search for these dimensions of Christian discipleship in a presumed transcendent and formal 'will of God'. That position I have set out above briefly, but I want now to pursue this question further.

The great Hebrew prophets of the 8th and 6th centuries BCE were profoundly right in their stern moral condemnation of personal and social immorality in ancient Israel. As a result of their work we have received an ethical vision and moral standards of great wisdom and enduring value. Given their historical context, the prophets naturally attributed the source of their moral judgments to the righteous will of Yahweh who was seen as angered by Israel's neglect of the Law. Among the prophets there were differing views concerning Yahweh's relationship to Israel, but they were all convinced that it was necessary for Yahweh to punish the nation for her faithlessness. They frequently claimed that Israel's experiences of oppression under neighbouring imperial powers were manifestation of Yahweh's justified wrath. Building on earlier centuries of evolution in religious understanding, Israel under the prophets embraced the notion of their God as deeply offended and necessarily punitive in relation to Israel's faithlessness.

This development represented an important advance in the religious awareness of ancient Israel. However, with hindsight born of the life and work of Jesus of Nazareth, we can see that centuries after the prophets developed their distinctive teaching about a punitive God it became a stumbling block in the evolution of human spiritual understanding.

Jesus of Nazareth, like his prophetic forbears, was a man of his own time. He too appears to have believed that his ethical vision and moral standards issued from the righteous divine will and purpose. But in his unwavering emphasis on the divine Loving as active and unconditional, and especially in his actions at the time of arrest and trial as represented by the New Testament evangelists, Jesus introduced a revolution into ancient Israel's spiritual legacy. This revolution concerns the human experiences of guilt, contrition and forgiveness.

In broken human relationships involving fault on one side, we may hope and anticipate that forgiveness will be extended by the person who has been wronged to the person who has done the wrong. But when there is a significant wrong-doing *and the apparent victim does not feel wronged and does not accuse the offender*, where does this leave the offender? For the victim, forgiveness is not necessary. But if the offender is suffering a guilty conscience, how can s/he be healed and move on to become a better person?

In the passion narratives of the four gospels, Jesus of Nazareth does not accuse of wrong-doing the people who have refused his vision and message and are preparing to trash his body. *He does not make them his enemies, and they feel no need for his forgiveness.* If there is to be a good result from this situation, something different from forgiveness is required from Jesus and something different from indifference and hostility is required in his accusers.

We see this 'difference' in Jesus as an unquenchable desire for them TO BECOME TRANSFORMED PERSONS. His burning wish is for them to be delivered of their present alienation from himself and from his God who is also their God. Previously Jesus had taught clearly and unequivocally that his God is not alienated from humanity by our wrong-doing. In Jesus' teaching - as in his suffering of body and mind on the cross - he affirms that the single work of Sacred Presence is the act of Loving which seeks to gather all people to Itself. The unconditional Loving that Jesus affirms seeks to deliver human life from immorality and ugliness and in their place to create righteousness and beauty. The goal is transformation of people. This is the most profound meaning of the divine Loving which was active in Jesus and which continuously surges throughout the world as the gift of Sacred Presence.

But in this situation the plotters make no response to Jesus' silent suffering. They pursue their plans to the end. What Jesus does in his life and death became important for a host of other people who were not present on that fateful day. For most of those present we have no record of a change of heart.

A classic tale which helps us to understand the depths and significance of the crucifixion scene is presented by Victor Hugo in his famous story, "Les Miserables". When we meet the central character, Jean Valjean, he has just become a free man after having served nineteen years in the galleys for a minor offense. But everywhere he goes he is scorned and rejected because he is required by law to identify himself as an ex-convict. Only at the modest village home of a humble bishop is he welcomed.

For the first time in years Jean Valjean is fed an excellent meal and given a comfortable bed - though he is careful to observe the valuable silver service laid out on the dining room table. After retiring for the night he steals the silver and runs off. He is apprehended by the police and taken back to the house. But the bishop makes no accusation. He tells the police that the silver pieces were a gift from himself to the man. He also observes that Valjean neglected to take two valuable candlesticks that he had also been given and which the bishop now places in Valjean's hands. The apprehended man is free to go. Victor Hugo, in the text, makes it abundantly clear the bishop acts from a humble, loving heart and only with concern for a man who deparately needs to be accepted and helped.

Jean Valjean, in his ensuing mental and spirirtual turmoil, begins to recognize and to accept for himself the transforming power of the love that has been offered to him by the bishop. As he wanders about in a distracted state, he cries out in sorrow and self-accusation for his ungrateful heart. And later he is able to begin a new and creative life in service of others, a life that unfolds in the rest of the story.

What happened to Jean Valjean? His theft had filled him with guilt and fear. Guilt - because he had stolen the bishop's property. Fear - because he knew that he could not defend himself against the accusations that he believed would be coming from the bishop and the police. The threat of being returned as a prisoner to slavery in the galleys for the rest of his life was a ghastly prospect.

Two events reversed his situation. First, he was not accused by the bishop but was affirmed as a worthwhile human being able to receive love. And this permitted something else to happen: he began to recognize that failure, guilt and sorrow are necessary parts of being a whole person. The classical term for this total awareness is 'contrition': "I have failed, I am guilty, I am sorry." True contrition comes to us as a gift of unconditional Loving, and it issues in repentance - the resolve to live in better ways in the future. This process is at the heart of spiritual transformation. And transformations - from the smallest and least noticed, to ones that are major - are at the heart of the spiritual journey. The process of transformation is the constant healing and renewing of the human person, in response to the unconditional Loving of Sacred Presence mediated through the Truth, Beauty and Goodness of Earth, her people and other creatures.

In my reading of the gospels of the New Testament I do not find Jesus of Nazareth acting as the agent of a punitive God who accuses humanity of wrong-doing. I see him intending by word and deed to revolutionize the spiritual understanding and practice of the faith tradition of his people. Most of the new Christian church, however, failed to understand this. The emerging church readily assumed the institutional role of divinely-appointed prosecutor of unrighteous humanity on behalf of an offended and punitive God. Church doctrines proclaimed a God whose wrath is only averted through the sacrificial death of the divine Son, and this teaching became the linchpin of a tragic misreading of the meaning of Jesus' life and death. (I dealt extensively with the historic roots of this misreading in my book, "Sacred Presence".)

This misreading has had more deadly consequences for the world than can be recounted here. Through the self-righteous condemnation of people considered to be 'fallen' and 'sinful', the institutional church rationalized its ruthless persecution of 'heretics' in the Middle Ages. The same rationalization was used to justify the imperial ambitions of Dutch and Belgian Christian nationals in the Far East and Africa, of Spanish and Portugese conquistadores in Central and South America, and of French and English settlers in North America. In each case 'pagan savages' were discounted and destroyed because of their presumed 'unredeemed' state. And, sadly, modern versions of the same false teaching persist today in parts of the church throughout the world.

This misreading of the meaning of Jesus' life and death has also allowed so-called Christian nations to accept war and military preparations for war as consistent with the Christian faith. Many devoted church members have not understood the radical non-violence in Jesus' life and death, and have failed to affirm the centrality of the divine Loving mediated by people as necessary for the health of the world. Surely this extended tragedy has been for Jesus a constant crucifixion, and for the Holy One a sorrow beyond our imagining.

Fortunately, there have always been other Christian voices who have not made this misreading. There has always been a 'prophetic impulse' in the church to demonstrate the Way of contrition, repentance and transformation enabled by the divine Loving. This is the path of true discipleship. The God whom Jesus embraced and announced in word and deed loves actively and unconditionally. 'Grief and compassion' - not anger and punishment - is the appropriate way to speak of the divine response to human frailty and wrong-doing. The Holy One does not claim to be 'wronged' by us but instead responds to our moral struggles with gifts which can enable our spiritual transformation.

What can be meant, then, by the phrase, the "forgiveness of God", if in our understanding and faith we move beyond the image of a God who is offended, wrathful and punitive? Then the traditional notion that humanity needs God's forgiveness - a belief commonly held - dissolves into the theological detritus of the past. Bonhoeffer called the easy religious dispensation of divine forgiveness 'cheap grace'. Perhaps this is an aspect of 'religion' that he hoped 'religionless Christianity' would leave behind.

On the other hand, we ourselves need to be forgiving persons because we so easily take offence, feel resentment, and make accusations when others do us wrong. The effort to go beyond our own hurt and to extend forgiveness to the other person is 'costly grace'. It is testimony to the divine Loving working in us to bring reconciliation and healing into human relationships. And this effort of reconciliation is part of 'the grace of transformed living' that can be ours only by the 'costly' spiritual endeavours of contrition and repentance.

Jesus of Nazareth is reported to have said, "Love your enemies, do good to those who hate you, bless those who curse you, pray for those who abuse you." To live the meaning of Jesus' words we require a wisdom and generosity that goes goes beyond seeing ourselves and other people as forgiven sinners. Rather, we must understand that all of us are wounded and broken persons needing the healing work of love.

A NEW PARADIGM

The Hebrew, Christian and Islamic religions teach that their God is the Holy and Righteous One who judges humanity for its sin. This belief has deep roots in a profound sense of awe which from earliest times humans experienced in response to the powerful mysteries within and surrounding their lives. This feeling of awe in response to cosmic reality took the form over the ages of an existential terror, an emotion which became focused and sublimated in many different ways within the sacred rites of institutionalized religion.

In the foundational tradition of the ancient Hebrews the feeling of awe merged with a sense of moral fault which they were able to express in the term 'sin'. They developed the belief that Yahweh's righteous wrath against sin required specific acts of propitiation, of atonement, in order for his People to feel able to approach Him.

But Jesus of Nazareth challenged this belief and practice. He taught and lived so fundamental a change in the human/Divine relationship that only in recent times are some parts of humanity finally beginning to break free from the suffocating hold which the divine Judge of the Abrahamic religions have had on human imagination and behaviour. In Jesus of Nazareth we learn that the Sacred Presence responds to our faults only and always with absolute and unconditional loving. No condemnation is made and no forgiveness is necessary because no offense has been endured. Instead we learn that in the Holy One there is a profound grieving. And we see also in Jesus a generous divine grace holding out to us the hope and the possibility and the means of spiritual transformation which can enable moral living.

The traditional religious paradigm taught us to ask of God, "Forgive us our sins". The new paradigm of spiritual life says, "The notion of people as 'sinners before the Holy' is a human invention, a label and burden mistakenly laid upon us by religious tradition. Sacred Presence names everyone 'the beloved' and labours quietly and continually within us to reveal to each one her or his own Truth." This in no way denies that human moral fault is a ubiquitous and destructive force but it affirms the Sacred as our healing Companion in the Journey.

The traditional religious paradigm says to God, "Thy will be done". The new paradigm of spiritual life says to us, "Seek, discover and enter into your own Truth and you will learn that there are gifts of the Spirit to be received for your personal formation and reformation."

Finally, the new paradigm of spiritual life affirms that in human social relationships the gift of true forgiveness from one person to another is a 'costly grace'. In the face of a significant wrong endured, true forgiveness seeks reconciliation with the offender through a redeeming intention: "I am sorry for being so quick to rebuke you and so slow to love you. In the future I will make a greater effort to see and love the person you truly are".

To know the grace of this forgiveness - either in the giving or in the receiving - is to touch the Heart of everything.

A NEW STORY

By the year 800, the Christ Story and its biblical world view had been established as the grand, compelling narrative of salvation in Western civilization. At that time the Christian church entered into a contest with the secular Holy Roman Empire to determine which institution would be the dominant power in Europe. And, while that battle was never formally resolved, for the next 1000 years the church and its Story provided the fundamental texture of the culture. The decline of that Story in the last 500 years has been the result of two forces of increasing significance, beginning in the time of the European Renaissance.

The first undermining force has been the scientific method. The historic church grounded its authority in the Holy Scriptures. Accepting those sacred writings as foundational and as revealed truth, Christian theology - designated Queen of the sciences - used deductive reasoning to carry implications of the Christian story into every corner of life. (Deductive reasoning starts from fixed assumptions and develops logical consequences which are applied wherever they seem appropriate.)

Beginning in the 16th century an increasing discrepancy appeared between the teachings that theology offered and the information supplied by the inductive method of science. The inductive method collects data by observation and from controlled experiments, and then uses logical analysis and intuitive judgment to reach conclusions. Using this method, science demonstrated that much of the church's teaching about the natural order and about human nature is not tenable. The grand, compelling Story of the centuries was being undermined, for the most part unintentionally.

The second force in this subversive work was the emergence of a rival salvation mythology which has gradually won worldwide allegiance. From the 16th century onwards, material wealth in increasing quantities was taken into Europe from foreign lands to support the rise of an industrious and prosperous bourgeoisie. This class fostered the secular ideology of material and spiritual 'progress'. Moreover, scientific data began to accumulate which supported an evolutionary hypothesis for the continuing progressive development of Earth and all its creatures. In the late 19th century, this hypothesis was extended to human social life, thus strengthening a secular vision of inevitable social and economic progress. Gradually human life began to be seen as an indefinite progression of intellectual understanding and material wealth, a 'salvation' without end. The future seemed limitlessly wonderful, leaving the classical Christian world view weakened and sidelined in comparison with the secular vision of indefinite progress.

There is no close parallel in the Asian world to the European cultural evolution of the last 500 years, but the same two forces of the scientific method and the rise of a secular ideology of progress have gradually inserted themselves into Eastern cultures as well. As a result, the late 20th century phenomenon of 'globalization' has become the context of spiritual crisis and conflict that is worldwide.

The thoroughly secularized narrative of indefinite progress has generated a spreading consensus about what is 'real' and 'worthwhile' which is challenging all of humanity's traditional sacred stories. Moreover, this secular consensus is still gaining ground in spite of the obvious and glaring inadequacy of the current results of 'progress', an inadequacy evident in the widespread dysfunctioning of world society and a seriously wounded Earth.

The contest is on. The secular ideology of progress presses forward through an ability to persuade people that material possessions bring the good life.

> The genius of contemporary capitalism is not simply that it gives consumers what they want, but that it makes them want what it has to give. It's that core logic of ever-expanding desires that is unsustainable on a global scale.
> (T.G. Ash, "CCPA Monitor").

Can people of spiritual conviction successfully expose the dangers of the secular ideology of progress and offer a sane and sound alternative? Only, I suggest, if the traditional teaching and practice of all that we call 'religion' has a thorough overhaul.

For the world to survive mounting ecological, economic and political crises, the life journey of contemporary people needs new spiritual, ethical and moral foundations. Spiritual enquiry seeks to explore the meaning of Sacred Presence as the basis and guiding Light of our existence. Ethics derives from spiritual truth, concerns itself with general principles of human conduct, and is visionary. Moral standards derive from ethical vision and specify what is right and what is wrong for daily human behaviour. In all three fields of enquiry we must discern what is to be valued and carried forward from received traditions of the past. We must also take up the work of discovering new spiritual and moral paths which are consistent with our membership in the cosmos. Eventually, it is to be hoped, humanity will have fashioned from these and other endeavours a new grand, cross-cultural and compelling Story for all of humankind.

MORAL PERIL AND SIGNS OF HOPE

Our moral peril as a global society is everywhere apparent. Recall, for example, the steady militarization of Europe, North America and Asia, and the universal power and destructive influence of the military-industrial complex. Highly profitable research into and manufacture of increasingly sophisticated weapons have spawned a huge industry of death. All future wars will tear up the earth, pollute the atmosphere, and massacre people with destructive consequences such as never before experienced. We have become a violent society which, if unreformed, can only lead to the demise of Earth as we have known it.

Moreover, while wealthy nations waste these enormous sums of money on armaments and munitions, only paltry amounts are spent on correcting widespread and growing poverty and other forms of serious social malaise. As a result, there is desperate poverty among at least one third of the world's population while less than one tenth becomes obscenely wealthy.

Traditional moral values have become confined to the limited space of hearth and home, leaving general social life without direction or moral purpose. Our public policies and actions betray the spiritual rootlessness of society. Thomas Berry ("Evening Thoughts") describes the extent of the challenge we face:

> The universe is primarily a communion of subjects, not a collection of objects. Those of us who live in the industrial world have become locked into ourselves, into the human process. We cannot relate to the outer world in any effective manner. We cannot get out, and the outer world cannot penetrate the human. We have lost our reverence, our sense of mystery, our sense of the sacred. We do not hear the voices - the voices of the surrounding world, the voices of the entire range of natural phenomena.

"We have lost our reverence, our sense of mystery, our sense of the sacred." And what shall we do to recover from this terrible alienation? Berry believes that a creative future for humankind is possible through a renewed understanding of and appreciation for the sacredness of Nature in its cosmic reach. Especially here, in this rich Earth - in her beauty and wisdom and generosity - are gifts that we need so that we can take our part in the continuing Story of the cosmos. Here we can discover Sacred Presence among us as both hidden and disclosed. Here, in this wondrous Earth home, are foundations for a renewed spirituality which can reach into every aspect of personal and social life to bring purification, healing and transformation.

The most powerful and consistent demands for a new social righteousness in our world, for a new social contract, are not be found among the rich and famous. They are to be found among the poorest and most oppressed people, many of whom claim to speak in the name of a Righteous God. Out of their misery and wretchedness they often discern with great clarity the root causes of the injustices which deny them their human needs and rights. The pronouncements of the annual World Social Forums of recent years, for example, have echoed with insights and demands which blaze out with prophetic acuteness and urgency. The Uruguayan poet, writer and social critic, Eduardo Galeano, says that "the Future has a way of coming from the Edges."

The phenomenal rise in the last couple of decades of Non Governmental Organizations (NGOs) testifies to widespread discontent with the performance of every senior government with respect to a variety of social issues. Citizen groups have formed to lobby government on questions of poverty, civil rights, the environment, the arms industries, homelessness, the hungry. There are widespread feelings of a need to create justice in all human relationships as a basis for true and lasting peace in our homes, communities, nations and among nations.

At the centre of the present search for a righteous social order is the work of articulating a New Story which can belong and bring liberation to all people. The traditional sacred stories which for centuries have guided the different parts of humanity are proving to be inadequate for the challenges of a converging and presently stifling global culture. The future New Story is emerging through a new cosmology which articulates humanity's common ancestry in the evolution of Earth and all her creatures. It appears within the demands of millions of people for a universal justice that can provide the basis for a lasting peace. And the New Story is also being shaped within the personal spiritual journeys of people who respond to the inner demands of their own lives.

In the results of this spiritual alchemy, working within all these disparate and yet unified elements, lies our hope for the future.

Questions for Discussion

In what ways do you express your sense of Sacred Presence?

If you have been seeking more adequate images of the Sacred, what has this yielded for you?

What important insights for your journey do you draw from the New Cosmology?

To what extent is an awareness of the immanence of the Sacred important for your spiritual journey?

To what extent is an awareness of the divine initiative important for your spiritual journey?

What are the contents of your ethical vision?

What moral failures of our society trouble you most? for what reasons?

What factors and forces presently support you most successfully in this "groping phase" (Thomas Berry's expression) of humanity's spiritual journey?

epilogue

Sacred Presence
  hidden
  within each
  ripple of air
  tremour of waters
   mountain and plain
crowds into my small soul

embraced by your Presence
wakened to new possibilities
let me not be anxious
but in gratitude yield

mottled evening sky
beckons to soul work
which is there
waiting
deeper than my reach
waiting
for the breath of the Sacred

    how much space do I need
       do you need?
    will you help me to occupy my space
       I help you to occupy yours?
    when my space and your space meet
       will we enlarge or diminish each other?

I try to stay poised
focused
grounded
but news from the world
clips me broadside
my balance fails
I stagger
crash

                Jesus goes into Galilee
                seeks out
                pain   confusion   fear
                offers
                healing   truth   love
                in
                the present moment

APPENDIX

In my book "Sacred Presence: in Search of the New Story", I suggested that changes were needed in liturgies used when Christians and their friends gathered. Some readers were interested to know what form the Eucharist might take to reflect such changes. I responded with a possible text, variants of which have been used occasionally and have received positive response. I set it out here hoping that it will serve a wider audience. It is experimental and is intended to invite modifications to reflect local interests and needs. It may be copied/adapted without permission.

NOTES FOR AN ALTERNATIVE LITURGY

Communal meals are a kind of ritual both formal and informal, and are as old as humanity. They provide familiar and welcome contexts for human social interaction. Certain communal meals included elements which invited participation by the Sacred. The Christian Eucharist is one such meal.

The Eucharistic ritual is a sacred drama in which all those present are the actors. The role of the Presider is to help us to be at ease and able to take our parts in the ceremony. Traditionally this role has been reserved for an ordained person. But in special circumstances a community might decide to select one of their own members for this responsibility.

The drama opens with a recital of cosmic origins. Then follows 'Instruction'. The Presider invites us to open our minds and hearts to the readings, not all of which need be taken from the Bible since there is a large treasury of appropriate writings available to us.

The community then turns to 'Recollection' focussed on certain aspects of Christian living, and to 'Prayers of the People' which should be specific and contain invitations to action.

The 'Sacramental Meal' takes us to the heart of our celebration where we remember the life and work of Jesus of Nazareth, and share in the sacramental gifts.

The liturgy ends with a solemn dismissal, urging us to take into daily living the healing, wisdom and blessing we have received.

THE CHRISTIAN EUCHARIST
an alternative rite

Gathering

A Song gathers the community

Presider: In the beginning, Sacred Presence.
In the beginning, the Source of all that is.

Congregational responses are in bold print

In the beginning, primordial Energy flaring forth in creative ecstasy, yielding space and time.

P: A Universe surging forth in clouds of cosmic dust, declaring a Mystery of Holiness:

The Sacred yearning, moaning, labouring, giving birth, rejoicing.

P: Myriad creatures born in the longing of the Holy One; and humanity, one of the beloved.

*In small assemblies, a gong is sounded
in large assemblies, musicians sound cymbal and fanfair*

P: We praise You, divine Creator for the magnificence of the Cosmos, resplendent in expanding space and time, galaxies and stars, comets and planets, and Earth our island home.

For brother Sun and sister Moon;
for mountains and plains, seas and lakes and rivers;
for insects, reptiles and fish, birds and animals,
flowers and trees and edible plants;
and for all the teeming life around us.

P: We praise You, Holy Wisdom,
   for the rich diversity of Earth's peoples and cultures;
   for the nurture and companionship of home and community;

For the journey of Christian discipleship into which You call us; for spiritual gifts which sustain us in Jesus's Way of caring and compassion, of justice and peace.

P: We praise You, Indwelling Presence,
   for the inner Light of your Spirit,
   for gifts of listening and speaking, of dreaming and creating,
   for this time of word and song, prayer, sacrament,
                                    and shared silence.

Sacred Presence:
hidden, and yet disclosed in your mighty acts;
help us to accept all that You desire to give us this day.
In the Holy Name of Jesus we pray.   AMEN

A Song of thanksgiving

Instruction

P: Let us be still in body and alert in mind

We desire to be open to the Gift of Wisdom
       through words to be read for our instruction

   Each reading is introduced with brief explanatory comments

READER: This reading comes from ....
         Listen in heart and mind for the Living word.

   After each reading there is a pause, and this exchange:

READER: Hear what the Spirit is saying to the church;
May our hearts be open to the Living Word.

All readings concluded, there is a short time for reflection. Then, with a minimum of movement, pairs form in the assembly to share insights gleaned from the readings. After an appropriate length of time the Presider calls the community together again. On special occasions, there may be a sermon in place of sharing. At the conclusion of this time, the Presider continues:

P: The Living Word comes to those who journey with an
 honest heart and open mind

We seek the Light of Truth for our world, shining in the hearts of those who work for justice and peace.

A Song - related if possible to one of the Readings

Recollection

A brief time of silence is kept after each Bidding

P: We remember that we are pilgrims of the Way who journey with the companionship and blessing of the Sacred Presence...

We remember the need for healing of our soul wounds, of interior afflictions which injure us and persons close to us...

We remember our need of contrition and repentance for failure in moral living, and for grace to amend our lives...

We remember the need of provision for everyone of food, clothing and shelter, so that we may secure in our social life a fair distribution of material goods...

We remember our need for ecological awareness, and for respect and responsible action in relation to all Earth's creatures...

Sacred Presence, assist us each day to seek and to live in response to your guidance in our lives. Amen.

Prayer of the People

*Two or three persons will be assigned in the week preceding
to list current concerns for each subject specified below
and to lead in this time of prayer.*

We recall recent tragic events ....
Holy One, you are present in our grief. Comfort and sustain us so that we may engage in works of compassion and healing.

We remember persons in this community ....
    and in the world community ....
    and these tasks to be accomplished ....
Guide us so that our response to these persons and tasks may be wise and generous.

We give thanks for blessings ....
Teach us true gratitude that we may be witnesses to your loving kindness.

We remember our responsibilities in society ....
Enable us to be active in the works of justice and peace

Let us exchange with one another a sign peace -
    local custom determines how this is done

Peace be with you.
And also with you.

A Song

The Sacrament of Bread and Wine

P: Behold bread and wine, gifts of Earth and the fruit of human labour, to become for us Signs of New Life   *(the elements are elevated).*

   Thanks be to God.

Let us open our hearts.
   We open them to the Holy One.

Let us declare the divine Goodness.
   This is our hope and joy.

P: SACRED PRESENCE, throughout uncounted eons of the unfolding universe You have been its inner Truth and enabling Source.
The Created Order proclaims your Wisdom and your Generosity.
   A gong is sounded

Sacred Presence,
Source of life and love:
Galaxies, Stars and Earth show forth your glory.
Sing Hosanna, Sing Hosanna.
Blessed is the One whose Presence lightens our hearts.
Sing Hosanna, Sing Hosanna.

Gracious and Holy One, your wondrous generosity is evident for all to behold. But human hearts have been hard, human ways have been destructive, and the whole Creation groans with unfulfilled expectation.

To heal a broken world You raise up wise women and men in every generation. You spoke through Abraham an Sarah, Moses and Miriam, and through the prophets of ancient Israel and other sacred traditions.

In the fulness of time you sent Jesus of Nazareth to show us the Way of truth and love, of compassion, justice and peace. He healed the sick and shared himself with social outcasts. He challenged the corruption and evil in his world. Through his disciples he created a Servant Community.

Jesus was a prophet and wise servant of his people, radiant with the Mystery of Lowliness. Though powerful enemies rejected and killed him, Holy Love in him prevailed; his Truth and Love abide among us.

On the night before his trial and death on a cross, Jesus shared a meal with his friends. Out of the depths of his heart, out of the fulness of his love, he offered them bread and said,
   "This is my Body".

Then he took a cup of wine and shared it with them, saying
   "This is a Sign of the New Covenant".

Through sharing bread and wine we recognize the longing in our hearts for a time when humanity will live as one, and with respect and love for Earth and all her creatures.

The Presider elevates the bread and wine, and declares:

Know yourselves as disciples of Jesus.
Know yourselves as friends of God.

AMEN!   So be it.

The consecrated elements are distributed with these words:

RECEIVE THE BREAD OF NEW LIFE.   **Amen**
RECEIVE THE CUP OF NEW BEGINNINGS.   **Amen**

P: Let us prary.
   a time of shared silence

Lead our hearts to do your will,
Guide our journey, for our delight is to follow in your
$\qquad\qquad\qquad\qquad\qquad\qquad\qquad\qquad\qquad\qquad$**Way.**

As we have been gathered and nourished here,
let us go out to share what we have received.

As we have rejoiced in our companionship as disciples of Jesus,
let us go to others as signs of friendship and open
$\qquad\qquad\qquad\qquad\qquad\qquad\qquad\qquad\qquad\qquad$**community.**

Go with peace, love and gratitude in your hearts.
Our liturgy has ended, our service begins.

THANKS BE TO GOD !

BIBLIOGRAPHY

Berry, Thomas. 1988. The Dream of the Earth.
                              Sierra Club, San Francisco.

Berry, Thomas. 2006. Evening Thoughts.
                              Sierra Club Books.

Bonhoeffer, Dietrich. 1964. Letters and Papers from Prison.
                              Collins (Fontana Books).

Chesterton, G.K. 1960. St. Francis of Assisi.
                              Hodder & Stoughton.

Eiseley, Loren. 1971. The Firmament of Time.
                              Atheneum.

_____ 1977. Another Kind of Autumn.
                              Scribner's.

Goodenough, Ursula. 1998. The Sacred Depths of Nature.
                              Oxford University Press.

Hafiz. 1999. The Gift.
                              Daniel Ladinsky, tr. Penguin Compass.

Herman, Emma. 1923. The Finding of the Cross.
                              James Clarke, London.

Julian of Norwich. 1978. Showings.
                              Colledge & Walsh, eds. Paulist Press.

Kelly, Thomas. 1941. A Testament of Devotion.
                              Harper & Bros.

May, Gerald. 2004. The Dark Night of the Soul.
                              HarperSanFrancisco.

E. Roberts & E. Amidon, eds. 1991. Earth Prayers.
                              HarperSanFrancisco.

Swimme, B. and Berry, T. The Universe Story. HarperSanFrancisco.

The Monitor. Canadian Centre for Policy Alternatives, April 2007

Walrus Magazine. July/August 2007

ISBN 142513799-7